hide this spanish book

Apa Publications GmbH and Co. Verlag
New York   Munich   Singapore

Contacting the Editors
Every effort has been made to provide accurate information in this publication, but changes are inevitable. The publisher cannot be responsible for any resulting loss, inconvenience or injury. We would appreciate it if readers would call our attention to any errors or outdated information; please contact us: Apa Publications, 193 Morris Avenue, Springfield, NJ 07081, USA. E-mail: hidethisxtreme@langenscheidt.com

First Printing: December 2009
Printed in Singapore

Publishing Director: Sheryl Olinsky Borg
Senior Editor/Project Manager: Lorraine Sova
Writer: Teresa Caro
Reviewer: Alejandra Gritsipis
Interior Design and Composition: Wee Design Group
Cover Design: Claudia Petrilli
Illustrator: Tatiana Davidova
Production Manager: Elizabeth Gaynor
Interior Photos: page 10, © 2009 Jupiterimages Corporation; page 87, © Ovidiu Iordachi 2009 Used under license from Shutterstock.com, © 2009 Jupiterimages Corporation, © Bernd Güssbacher 2009 Used under license from Shutterstock.com, © bramalia 2009 Used under license from Shutterstock.com, © Amy Nichole Harris 2009 Used under license from Shutterstock.com

INSIDE

INTRO

Which would you say or text to your BFF?

a. Hello, would you like to attend a party tonight?
b. Hey dude/bitch, wanna hang out 2nite?

If you picked option a, close this book now (we're warning you!). But, if you picked b, keep on reading...

This book is not for people who want to sound like they just got off the plane when they visit a Spanish-speaking country. It should be used only by cool people who want to learn how to speak real Spanish. There are no verb conjugations, no grammar lessons and no rules with all kinds of exceptions. The language included in this book is what young, hip Spanish speakers really say today, and we've made it as easy as possible for you pick up and use. You'll navigate your way through everything from dating and sex to fashion and style.

WHAT YOU NEED TO KNOW

We're assuming that you may already know a little Spanish, but it's OK if you don't. The expressions included in this book are translated with their closest equivalent in English—there isn't always a direct translation. We explain everything you need to know, and you can even hear some of the expressions in this book at our website, www.langenscheidt.com/hidethis. Look for: 🔊 . So, you don't only know what to say, but how to say it!

You may just want to listen to them with headphones so you don't offend anyone...

SEX

Got your attention? Words or expressions followed by ♂ are for guys only and those with ♀ are for girls only.

BOMBS AWAY!

We've labeled the really bad stuff clearly to try and save you from some uncomfortable situations. Here's how it works:

💣* means that you can use these words around your friends and sound cool;
💣*💣* are used for words that are completely inappropriate, incredibly offensive and downright dirty! You should only use these words with your closest friends and definitely not around Spanish old folks, teachers, etc.

FEATURES

You'll also notice these different features throughout the book:

Manga — Cool comics that features cool Spanish language

 — Conversations between Spanish hipsters

Word Bytes — A list of key words from the manga or dialogue

 — Short sentences, phrases or words for a lot of crazy situations

 — The best of the best—the shortlist of the hottest things

 — Fun activities that get you using the slanguage you've picked up

 — Interactive quizzes that test your personality and knowledge of Spanish slang

 — A Spanish-English game that lets you LOL while practicing your Spanish

Q&A — Our very own cultural and language advice column

For when you want to be naughty or nice

Know-it-all/Sabelotodo — Interesting facts on Spanish slang and culture from our resident nerd named Sabelotodo, which means "know-it-all" in Spanish!

Gestures — How to say it—visually

The best slang is often regional. For example, *bolsa* can mean bag in Mexico, but say it in the Dominican Republic and you'll get slapped—it's a vulgar way to call someone an imbecile.

Country-specific terms include a flag:

Argentina		Honduras	
Bolivia		Mexico	
Chile		Nicaragua	
Colombia		Peru	
Costa Rica		Puerto Rico	
Cuba		El Salvador	
Dominican Republic		Spain	
Ecuador		Venezuela	

DISCLAIMER

There are plenty of phrases in this book that can get you slapped, beat up or smacked down, but there are also plenty of things that can help you make new friends or fall in love with that special someone. It's all about how you decide to use the book. Just don't say we didn't warn you!

AND LAST BUT NOT LEAST...

Languages are constantly evolving—what's in today might be out tomorrow—and while we've done our best to give you the coolest and most up-to-date slang, it's possible that some of the expressions might go out of fashion. So, if you come across anything in this book that's outdated, or if you learn a cool new expression that you think we should include in the future, we'd love to hear from you! Send us an e-mail at: hidethisxtreme@langenscheidt.com.

chapter 1

Cool!

Get info on:

- different ways to say cool
- how to say something sucks

That's cool!

Know-it-all/Sabelotodo

"Cool" or "cold"—as in temperature—in Spanish is **frío**. Don't use this literal translation to mean "cool" as above.

 All That Slang

Although you can say *cool* in Spanish, here are some other, more authentic, words you can also use.

chévere	**estupendo**
tremendo	**chulo**
impresionante	

How to say cool in…

🌑 **legal**

🌑 **bacano**

🌑 **chimba**

🌑 **padre** *literally, father (Freud would have a blast with this one)*

🌑 **brutal** *literally, brutal*

🌑 **bacán**

🌑 **guay**

Use It or Lose It!

To express coolness, use these phrases. Just add the cool word of choice.

¡Eso está _____!

¡Qué _____!

¡Está demasiado _____!

¡Eso está bien chévere!
That is really cool!

¡Qué cool!
How cool!

¡Eso está cabrón! 💣
This is fucking great!

¡Qué cabrón! 💣💣
How fucking cool!

Q&A

Querida Paquita:
Last month I went to my cousin's house in Puerto Rico. We were talking about Madonna's latest video and how the singer Alejandra Guzman from Mexico wanted to be like her. My cousin kept repeating over and over again "That video *está demasia'o*". I don't understand what he meant, since *demasiado* means too much. I don't get it, it's too much *what*?!
Sincerely,
Desesperado (Desperate)

Querido Desesperado:
Don't fuss, *está demasiado* (or *demasia'o*) means it's "too good" or "off the hook". It's like saying something is so great, there isn't a word good enough to describe it. So, learn the phrase and use it.
Saludos,
Paquita

Querida Paquita:
The other day, a Spanish-speaking classmate told me I was very *chula*. When I looked up the word in an online dictionary, I found that *chulo* ♂ / *chula* ♀ means pimp or prostitute! What does it really mean?
Yours,
Ofendida (Offended)

Querida Ofendida:
Mantén la calma. Chulo ♂ / *chula* ♀ also means "nice" or "cool"—so you received a compliment! You may have heard the phrase *¡Qué chulin!* which means "How nice". This phrase is retro, but apparently (like leggings) it's making a comeback.
Saludos,
Paquita

Know-it-all/Sabelotodo

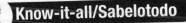

The expression "to keep your cool" can be translated as **mantener la calma/compostura**.

Dialogue: José y Katy

JOSÉ:	¡Hola, Katy!	Hello, Katy!
KATY:	¡Hola, José!	Hello, José!
JOSÉ:	**Te ves muy guay…**	You're looking *guay*…
KATY:	**¿GUAY?** (she slaps him)	*GUAY?*
JOSÉ:	**Pero… Katy… Guay significa cool.**	But…Katy… *Guay* means cool.
KATY:	**Oops, perdón… mala mía.**	Oops, sorry… my bad.
JOSÉ:	(to himself) **Menuda bofetada…**	What a lousy slap…

What do you think Katy understood?

Use It or Lose It!

How would you say cool if you were…?

1. in Mexico
2. in Spain
3. in Colombia
4. a potty mouth
5. a nice kid
6. in any Spanish-speaking place

1. padre; 2. guay; 3. bacano; 4. cabrón; 5. chévere; 6. chévere, tremendo, impresionante, chulo or cool—Remember you can never go wrong with cool, said with a Spanish accent, of course.

That's un-cool!

All That Slang

Of course, for every cool thing there is an un-cool thing. Here's how to say that something sucks.

Es una porquería.	It's garbage.
Menudo♂ /Menuda♀ porquería.	What a piece of crap. *You can also say **Menudo♂ /Menuda♀** + anything (car, work, person, etc.). It's a cynical remark, mainly used in Spain, implying something's no good.*
Charrería.	Garbage.
Está charro.	That's garbage. *Note that **charro** can mean silly, funny or small, in addition to un-cool.*
Está del carajo. 💣	It's shit.
¿Qué carajos es esta porquería? 💣	What the hell is this garbage?

11

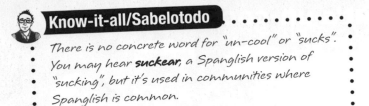
Use It or Lose It!

What's the right response for each situation? Don't mess up! (No pressure...)

a. Your best friend is showing off a brand-new MP3 player with voice recognition.

b. Your 67-year-old grandmother has been asked if she is pregnant by a 4-year-old.

c. Your best friend got you tickets to see your favorite band.

d. Your cousin slapped an old lady's ass.

e. Your friend has just been promoted.

1. **¡Qué brutal!**
2. **Te pasaste.**
3. **Guay.**
4. **¡Qué cool!**
5. **Manten la calma.**

1. e; 2. d; 3. c; 4. a; 5. b

Word Bytes

You're gonna need to know these for the quiz on the next page!

la abuelita	granny	**la familia**	family
el amigo	friend	**la fiesta**	party
la camiseta	T-shirt	**gracias**	thanks
en casa	at home	**la invitación**	invitation
cualquier cosa	anything	**el maratón**	marathon
el domingo	Sunday	**la película**	film
la esquina	corner	**la playa**	beach

Quiz Are you *guay*?

1. If invited to *una fiesta* you:
  a. check your calendar—you have a lot of *invitaciones*!
  b. say *gracias*, and then go home to watch a *película* with close *amigos*.
  c. go, sit in *la esquina*, then wonder why you went.

2. Your cell phone contact list has:
  a. so many people—including all the *amigos* you made while on spring break in Cancun—you don't remember half of them.
  b. good *amigos*, *familia* and the Chinese delivery phone number.
  c. your mom, grandma and aunt on speed dial.

3. Your favorite outfit is:
  a. whatever is in style now—and it always looks *brutal* on you.
  b. a classic outfit, like *vaqueros* and a *camiseta*. You always look clean.
  c. whatever you have on hand: sweat pants, oversized *camiseta*. *Cualquier cosa*.

4. Your favorite Spanish word for cool is:
  a. *cabrón* 💣 💣.
  b. *guay* or *chévere*.
  c. *espectacular*.

5. *Los domingos*, you'd rather:
  a. wake up and continue *la fiesta*.
  b. go to la *playa*, catch a *película* or enjoy a relaxing day *en casa* on your own.
  c. enjoy *un maratón de películas* of your choice with some of your friends.

Mainly A's: *cool*
You are so *guay* you are hot. But careful, some people might think you are too cool to be true!

Mainly B's: *chévere*
You may not be the life of the party, but you don't care and that makes you *guay*.

Mainly C's: *chulo*
Stop trying to be *guay*—enjoy yourself and others will enjoy spending time with you too. You are *chulo♂/chula♀* in your own way.

Use It or Lose It!

Off the top of your head—without looking back—name 10 cool and/or un-cool words you now know in Spanish. Write down your answers, then try reading your answers aloud in front of a mirror to see how *guay* (or un-*guay*) you look.

Friends & Family

chapter 2

Get info on:

- nicknames and pet names
- meeting people and talking with friends
- slang about family members

 All That Slang

Terms for strangers, acquaintances, friends and lovers…

tipo♂/tipa♀

🔴 man

🔵 tío♂/tía♀

🟢 chamo♂/chama♀

a typical guy/gal
Watch out—this can have a vulgar undertone when used sarcastically.

cabrón 💣✳

asshole

papi♂/mami♀

a hottie *(literally, daddy/mommy Many Spanish speakers use this in reference to their partner.*

socio ♂/socia ♀

 asere

🟦 **pana**

friend *literally, partner or associate*

niño ♂/niña ♀ bien
snob
This is said about a wealthy or stuck-up kid.

blanquito
richie *literally, whitey*
This has nothing to do with skin color, but is a disparaging term reserved for wealthy people.

aguacatón, jamón ♂/ aguacatona, jamona ♀

spinster *literally, avocado, ham*

🔴 **bobo-tonto**
gilipollas
dumbass

borrachón ♂/borrachona ♀
drunk

KEY: 🟦 Cuba 🟦 Puerto Rico 🔴 Spain   **15**

Use It or Lose It!

Can you find these people in this party scene? Good luck!

- **niña bien**
- **jamona**
- **mami**
- **borrachón**

Word Bytes

You gotta know these to take the quiz...

la abuelita	grandma	**el licor**	liquor
el baile	dance	**mucho♂/mucha♀**	a lot, much
la familia	family	**la música**	music
la fiesta	party	**la personalidad**	personality

Quiz What is your *personalidad*?

Are you a *niño* ♂/*niña* ♀ bien, *tío majo* ♂/*tía maja* ♀ or *borrachón* ♂/ *borrachona* ♀? Find out.

1. You're enjoying your day at *Playa Santa* beach on the south coast of Puerto Rico by:
   a. covering up with SPF 70 and an oversized T-shirt.
   b. playing beach volleyball with the *chicos y chicas guay* next to you. After the game, you and your new friends have a few drinks to celebrate.
   c. finding the perfect spot where suits are optional, then asking a *papi* or *mami* to rub oil on your back.

2. At *la fiesta de la familia*:
   a. your *abuelita* slips you some money for being so nice—you baked dessert and offered to drive a drunk aunt home.
   b. you bring some *sangría*, jump around with the *chamos* and leave early to meet your friends.
   c. you don't show up; you're tired of the family yapping about how you should get off your ass.

3. *La fiesta* is:
   a. a dinner party with your close friends, which you and your *mami* lovingly prepared together.
   b. getting together with friends, where the conversation is as important as the food and drinks!
   c. any place with *música, baile* and *mucho licor*…

4. *La fiesta* ends at:
   a. 10 o'clock, sharp—you need your eight hours (or more) of beauty sleep.
   b. 10, 11, 12, 1—it depends on the party…
   c. never!

Mainly A's: *niño* ♂/*niña* ♀ bien, borderline *bobo-tonto*
You want to be perfect and often forget to have fun. Still, you have a few good friends who really care about you. You won't get skin cancer, but you probably have an ulcer the size of Mexico.

Mainly B's: *tío majo* ♂/*tía maja* ♀
You are the life of the *fiesta*; everybody likes you! When you are not there, people notice it. Keep it up, but don't forget to get involved more deeply— you tend to have superficial relationships and often feel alone.

Mainly C's: *borrachón* ♂/*borrachona* ♀
You're too extreme. Still there is some hope if you quit being so sleazy. Also, consider getting strangers to rub some SPF 15 on your back instead of tanning oil.

All That Slang

When you're on a first name basis with Spanish speakers, try out some nicknames. Here are some of the most popular.

NAME	NICKNAME
Antonio	Toni, Toño
Cándida	Canda
Francisco	Paco
Isabel	Chabela
Javier	Javi
Jesús	Chu, Chuíto
Jesusa	Susa
José	Pepe, Che, Cheo
María	Mari
Milagros	Mili

Tato, Tito, Pito, Pepo, Papo are generic nicknames used regardless of the person's actual name. Diminutives are also often used; just add *-ito*♂ or *-ita*♀ to the end of the name, for example: Luis = Luisito; Carmen = Carmencita. Finally, if a guy has the same name as his dad, he may be affectionately called *Junito* (Junior).

Use It or Lose It!

What are these people's real names?

Cheo   Carmencita   Chu   Mari   Junito (Pepe's son)

Use It or Lose It!

Now, if you want to Spanish-sounding name, turn it into a diminutive. If your name ends in s, add *-ito*♂/*-ita*♀. If your name ends in a vowel sound, drop the vowel and add *-ito*♂/*-ita*♀. If your name ends with a consonant, other than s, add *-cito*♂/*-cita*♀. Try it...

Kenny	Kennito	Sandra	_____
Thomas	_____	your name here	_____
Jacklyn	_____		

Thomasito; Jacklyncita; Sandrita

◀ All That Slang

In case you forget someone's name, avoid embarrassment by using a pet name. Note: You'd be surprised how much people use—and abuse—pet names in Spanish, so don't be afraid to give it a try! You can also use these with your close friends and family.

cariño	darling	**mi vida**	my life
chulo ♂/chula ♀	sweetie	**papito ♂/mamita ♀**	hottie *literally, little daddy/mommy*
mi amor	my love		
mi corazón	my heart	**querido ♂/querida ♀**	dear

Querida Paquita:
On my last vacation I went to Argentina and a lot of people approached me with comments about the weather, the news, food, etc. I was afraid it was some kind of plot to steal my identity, so I snubbed them. I've discussed this with many friends and they said they would do the same. But recently, someone said I was paranoid and they were just being friendly. Whaddaya say about this?
Sinceramente, Jack

Querido Jack:
People in Latin America and Spain are warm and inviting (of course there are exceptions), and talking to strangers in the street is as normal as drinking coffee in the morning. So don't be afraid to chat with anyone. You don't even have to fear being asked for your mother's maiden name—it's common for Hispanics to use both their mother and father's last name. But don't give up your social security number.
Suerte, Paquita

Querida Paquita:
When I first met a friend from Guatemala, he gave me a kiss on the cheek. I found it weird, although I was a bit happy, because he obviously liked me. It turned out he is happily married and has no interest in me. When I met his wife, she gave me two kisses, one on each cheek. I haven't invited them to my house—I'm afraid they want a threesome. What should I do?
Asustada, Dolly

Querida Dolly:
Don't be a *gilipollas*. It's customary for Hispanics to kiss friends and family (and even strangers) as a greeting. Your friend's wife is most likely from Spain, where two kisses are planted with a lot of enthusiasm. You won't be expected to kiss anyone but, when someone kisses you, take it with grace. Also, don't be surprised if they call you *mi amor* or *querida*. Drop your guard and puck'r up (and don't be too quick to call your harassment lawyer).
Besos, Paquita

Use It or Lose It!

Finish this message using pet names.

_____ (my love), I just wanted to tell you that Jes and I have
decided to be together. Jes is _____ (my heart). Sorry,
_____ (my life), remember that you will always be my
_____ (darling), _____ (dear).

opɹǝnb ʻouᴉɹɐɔ ʻɐpᴉʌ ᴉɯ ʻuozɐɹoɔ ᴉɯ ʻɹoɯɐ ᴉɯ

●Dialogue: Chismes

Wanna gossip like the *chismosos* in this conversation?

RODRIGO:	**¿Te contaron?**	Did anybody tell you?
CATALINA:	**¿Qué?**	What?
RODRIGO:	**El tipo del apartamento de abajo tiene pareja nueva…**	The guy from the apartment below has a new partner…
CATALINA:	**¿De veras? ¿Cómo va a ser?**	Really? How so?
RODRIGO:	**Sí, me lo dijo Ángela. Y no te vas a imaginar quién es…**	Yes, Angela told me. And you will not believe who it is…
CATALINA:	**¿Quién?**	Who?
RODRIGO:	**¡El hermano de su ex novia!**	His ex-girlfriend's brother!
CATALINA:	**Dios mío, no lo puedo creer.**	OMG, I can't believe it.
RODRIGO:	**¡Qué bochinche!**	What a mess!

Word Bytes

el chisme	gossip (info)
chismear	to gossip
el chismoso/la chismosa	gossip (person)
el cuento	story
la mentira	lie
la nena	girl
qué	what
seguro ♂/segura ♀	sure
el vecino/la vecina	neighbor

Use It or Lose It!

Can you pass the polygraph? Write *verdadero* if the statement from the *chisme* is true, or *falso* if it's not.

1. In the beginning, Catalina does not believe what Rodrigo is telling her.
2. Catalina told Rodrigo the *chisme*.
3. The dude downstairs is dating someone new.

1. verdadero; 2. falso, Angela told the chisme to Rodrigo, and he told Catalina; 3. verdadero

 All That Slang

If you want to know more than you should, you must learn to gossip! Memorize these phrases to get what you want.

¿Qué pasó?	What happened?
¿Te enteraste?	Did you hear?
Me dijeron que...	They told me that...
No lo sabía.	I didn't know.
Escuché que...	I heard that...
¿Quién te dijo?	Who told you?

Use It or Lose It!

Finish this juicy bit of gossip.

HUMBERTO: Luisa, ¿_____? (Did you hear?)

LUISA: ¿_____? (What happened?)

HUMBERTO: Lo de Zoila… (The thing about Zoila…)

LUISA: _____. (No.)

HUMBERTO: Le chocó el carro al vecino. (She crashed the neighbor's car.)

LUISA: _____ (What a mess!)

Te enteraste; Qué pasó; No; ¡Qué bochinche!

Know-it-all/Sabelotodo

To know more about **chismes**, tune in to Spanish TV networks or websites like **Univisión**® and **Telemundo**®. These frequently air gossip shows. Watch and learn how to gossip like a pro—in Spanish!

Gestures

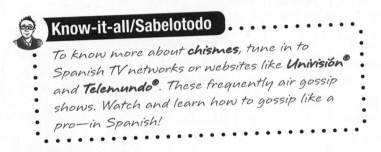

¿Qué? What? If you didn't understand, or if you want to know what somebody wants from you, move your nose up and down.

If you want to be confrontational, a slight forward chin movement is all you need to "say" ¡¿Qué carajos pasa?! (What the hell?!)

Daniel's dysfunctional family

¿¡Qué?!
What!?

¡Ay!
Ouch!

la abuela cool (tatuada)
cool (tattooed) grandma

el abuelo achacoso
achy grandpa

Yo cuido a mi familia.
I take care of my family.

Dónde están mis espejuelos?
Where are my glasses?

Salí a mi mamá.
I take after my mom.

Me encanta esta familia.
I love this family.

Nunca me he casado.
I've never been married.

la mamá tradicional
old-fashioned mom

el papá algarete
forgetful father

el tío rockero
rocker uncle

la tía ridícula
ridiculous aunt

la tía jamona
spinster aunt

Mi familia es la mejor.
My family is the greatest

¡QUIERO A MI MAMÁ!
I want my mommy!

No soporto a mi familia.
I can't stand my family.

¡Quiero vivir sola!
I want to live alone!

el hermano quejón
whiny brother

la prima antipática
arrogant cousin

la prima gótica
gothic cousin

Daniel
Daniel

Mixed Up

Try this grown-up version of fill-in-the-blank.

a. name for goth sister

b. name for hottie♂

c. name for arrogant brother

d. name for mindless mom

Carla, the _____ is waiting for her date to arrive. The doorbell rings.
            a

A _____ is at the door. Carla gets up to greet him, but is intercepted
      b

by _____. Diego, the _____, and the _____
         c   c   b

know each other! Then, the _____ walks in and says to her
                                    d

daughter, "I thought you had a date?!"

 All That Slang

Expand your slanguage on family members…

el mocoso/la mocosa

⟨ **el/la pibe**

⟨ **el/la chaval**

⟨•⟩ **el chavo/la chava**   kid

⟨ **el chamaco/la chamaca**

⟨ **el carajillo/la carajilla**

el viejo/la vieja   old man/old lady *These slang terms are used to talk about your parents.*

papi♂/mami♀   daddy/mommy *These terms are also used as pet names between a boyfriend and a girlfriend.*

pa ♂ /ma ♀	pa/ma *Just like in English*
el marido/la mujer	husband/wife *Not very PC, but still frequently used*
el abuelito/la abuelita	grandma/grandpa *You can also simply say **abu** to either.*
la titi	auntie

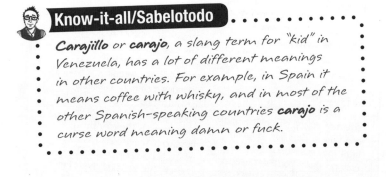

Know-it-all/Sabelotodo

Carajillo or *carajo*, a slang term for "kid" in Venezuela, has a lot of different meanings in other countries. For example, in Spain it means coffee with whisky, and in most of the other Spanish-speaking countries *carajo* is a curse word meaning damn or fuck.

Use It or Lose It!

Can you ID everyone in this family picture?

1. _____

2. _____

3. _____

4. _____

5. _____

6. _____

1. la chava; 2. el viejo; 3. la vieja; 4. el chavo; 5. la abuelita; 6. la abu

Q&A

Querida Paquita:

I'm dating a Mexican *tipo*; he's 24, very nice, handsome, polite and has a good job...but he still lives with his *vieja*! He doesn't come across as a momma's boy, but I just can't get over the fact that she still cooks him breakfast every morning. When's he gonna move out?

Saludos,
Jane

Querida Jane:

This is a very common situation among Hispanics—male and female. Kids live at home until they get married. It's a cultural thing. You'll get used to it, too, once his mom starts to spoil you as well!

Paquita

Querida Paquita:

I've been invited to a neighbor's *quinceañero*. What is it?!

Curious,
George

Querido George:

A *quinceañero* is the Latino version of a sweet 16 party. The celebration, which happens on a girl's 15th birthday, can be as big as a wedding; it includes a church ceremony, a beautiful dress and a grand party (including a sparkling cider toast). The only thing missing is the groom! Instead of exchanging rings at the church, the girl exchanges her flat shoes for new high heels, representing her coming into adulthood.

Paquita

Know-it-all/Sabelotodo

Spanish speakers from South America and the Dominican Republic address their parents with **usted** (formal you). Everywhere else, **tú** (informal you) is used when talking to parents.

Gay & Lesbian

chapter 3

Get info on:

- the usual and not so usual terms for "gay"
- gay-friendly phrases

All That Slang

Warning! These terms are insulting when used inappropriately.

♂ ♂ How to say "gay"…

maricón

farifo

 pato *literally, duck*

♀ ♀ How to say "lesbian"…

cachapera

tortillera

buchs *from the English word butch*

♂ ♀ How to say "transvestite"…

draga

estereosexual

la/el que pinta y raspa *literally, the one who paints and scrapes; meaning the person who fulfills two positions*

Know-it-all/Sabelotodo

Be PC and use these terms:
gay/homosexual, lesbiana, bisexual, transexual, travesti
No English translations needed, right?! All other terms can be highly offensive, except when used by those in the LGBT community.

KEY: ● Colombia ● Ecuador ● Nicaragua ● Puerto Rico ● Venezuela

Use It or Lose It!

What would you call these people? Write 'em down, *en español*.

1.

   _____

2.

   _____

3.

   _____

4.

   _____

1. tortilleras; 2. cachapera; 3. draga; 4. maricones

 Know-it-all/Sabelotodo

The rainbow flag is an international symbol of LGBT acceptance and hard to miss, no matter where in the world you stand. (But, be aware that in Bolivia, Ecuador and Peru, a rainbow flag is also used as a symbol of cultural identity for Andean civilization.)

In some parts of the Spanish-speaking world, homosexuals are openly accepted in their community. For example, in Oaxaca, Mexico, **muxe** (the local term for homosexuals) are an integral part of the community. In some other Spanish-speaking countries, taboos against homosexuality still exist.

El lío de faldas

Word Bytes

el lío de faldas

to have an affair *literally, skirt mess*

salir del clóset

come out of the closet *In some places you might hear **salir del armario**. **Armario** is the Spanish word for "closet".*

estar fuera del clóset

to be out of the closet

 Know-it-all/Sabelotodo

*Notice how the dog speaks Spanish! In Spanish, dogs say **jau** or **guau** (it sounds like "how" or "gwow"), not "bark" or "woof". Cats, on the other hand, say **miau**, which sounds exactly like the English "meow".*

Use It or Lose It!

Do you know what to say in these situations? Select from the phrases below.

1. You just found out… Jan plays for the other team!
2. You want to know how someone found out Jan plays for the other team.
3. You want to say, "What?!"
4. You want to tell people Jan is out, finally.

¿Cómo te enteraste?

Jan salió del clóset.

¿Qué? ¿Jan salió del clóset?

Miau.

¿Qué?

¿Cómo te enteraste?

1. ¿Qué? ¿Jan salió del clóset?
2. ¿Cómo te enteraste?
3. ¿Qué?
4. Jan salió del clóset.

Mixed Up

Put your new vocab to use. Use the LGBT terms to finish the text.

Name a:

a. term for lesbian   b. term for bisexual   c. term for gay

José and María broke up because María is a _____. She wanted

<u>   a   </u>

to date Desirée. But Desirée was really straight, not a _____ or

<u>   b   </u>

_____. After his failure with María, José thought he might try being

<u>   a   </u>

a _____.

<u>   c   </u>

Gesture

Put your fingers down, and make a wrist movement down, as if you were a dog giving your paw. You'll proclaim someone gay.

So gay!

🔊 All That Slang

If you're gay, some of these phrases may help you get lucky. If not, read on to be in-the-know on gay culture.

Mi mejor amigo♂/amiga♀ es gay.	My best friend is gay.
El es un *top*, el da.	He is a top, he gives.
El es un *bottom*, el recibe.	He is a bottom, he receives.
A mí me gusta abajo.	I like to be on the bottom.
Yo soy versátil.	I'm versatile.
Ella es el macho en la relación.	She is the man in the relationship.
Me gustan los osos.	I like bears. *Osos are atypical gay men who are often ungroomed and unshaven.*
El hombre es como el oso: mientras más peludo, más sabroso.	Man is like a bear: the more hair the better. *This phrase is not specifically gay, but boy is it appropriate for osos!*
Es una loca.	He is a crazy girl. *This is said of flamboyant men.*
Es ambiguo♂/ambigua♀.	He/She is ambiguous.
Tira para los dos lados.	She/He plays on both teams.
¿Dónde está la barra gay más cercana?	Where's the nearest gay bar?
¿Dónde hay una disco gay?	Where's a gay club?
¿Qué vas a hacer esta noche?	What are you doing tonight?
¿Dónde puedo encontrar un show de dragas?	Where can I find a drag show?
Ella/Él es su tape.	She/He is his/her cover.
Celebra tu orgullo gay.	Celebrate your gay pride.
Estoy orgulloso de ser gay.	I'm proud of being gay.

Know-it-all/Sabelotodo

Did you notice in some of the phrases above, the female form was used to describe a man? Spanish is a gender-specific language and, in the case of sexuality, speakers can change the gender forms to indicate femininity or masculinity.

Quiz

Do you come across as straight, gay or bi?

This quiz will help you uncover your true sexual nature.

1. You've just arrived at a trendy Spanish locale, visit the tourist office, and:
   a. ask the clerk: *¿Dónde está la barra gay más cercana?*
   b. ask a girl and then a guy: *¿Qué vas a hacer esta noche?*
   c. flirt with a clerk of the opposite sex.

2. In the historic part of the city, you notice that the nicest café has a rainbow flag sticker on the door. You:
   a. go in; you know you'll make friends with the cute waiters.
   b. walk in, look around, then walk out. Maybe you'll try the place next door, which has a mix of guys and girls enjoying drinks.
   c. avoid the place like the plague.

3. You arrive at the town's hottest shopping mall and:
   a. immediately locate the designer stores; you've gotta look as fashionable as the rest of 'em.
   b. you're torn between buying a tight, sexy shirt and a classic button-down. You end up getting both.
   c. invest in a classic outfit—much like the one you're wearing.

4. You finally meet that perfect someone for a fling. You've chosen:
   a. *una loca*, if you're a guy (you like your men girly) or *una lesbiana*, if you're a girl.
   b. a boy or a girl, *te da igual*.
   c. a member of the opposite sex, of course.

Mostly A's: homosexual
Estás muy orgulloso de ser gay. Enjoy the gay life, baby!

Mostly B's: bisexual
To some you are *ambiguo. Te da igual.* You like girls and boys.

Mostly C's: heterosexual
You're either straight or are so deep in the *armario.*

Q&A

Querida Paquita:
   I'm gay and going on vacation to Argentina with my partner. Is it safe for us to be ourselves in public?

Tuya,
Gata

Querido Gata:
   In most Spanish-speaking metropolitan cities, you can comfortably be gay. Also, don't be afraid to ask a young person where the hotspots are. Popular tourist destinations often offer great alternatives to the hetero scene, and the young locals know the best places to go.

Paquita

Use It or Lose It!

Did you pay attention? Do you really know what each phrase means? See if you can pair the phrase with its gay English equivalent.

1. **Celebra tu orgullo gay.**
2. **Mi mejor amigo es gay.**
3. **Ella es el macho en la relación.**
4. **Me gustan los osos.**
5. **Él es su tape.**

a) She's the man in the relationship.
b) My best friend is gay.
c) Celebrate your gay pride.
d) He is her cover.
e) I like bears.

1. c; 2. b; 3. a; 4. e; 5. d

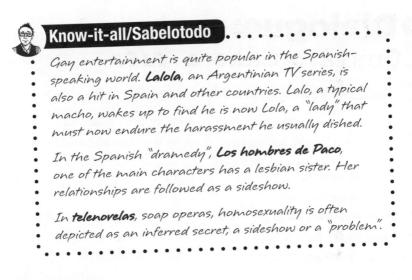

 **Know-it-all/Sabelotodo**

Gay entertainment is quite popular in the Spanish-speaking world. **Lalola**, an Argentinian TV series, is also a hit in Spain and other countries. Lalo, a typical macho, wakes up to find he is now Lola, a "lady" that must now endure the harassment he usually dished.

In the Spanish "dramedy", **Los hombres de Paco**, one of the main characters has a lesbian sister. Her relationships are followed as a sideshow.

In **telenovelas**, soap operas, homosexuality is often depicted as an inferred secret, a sideshow or a "problem".

A-List

Top-rated *películas gay*, gay-themed flicks…

A mi madre le gustan las mujeres	My Mother Likes Women
Antes de que anochezca	Before Night Falls
No se lo digas a nadie	Don't Tell Anyone
Lucas me quería a mí	Lucas Loved Me
Cachorro	Cub

Love & Dating

Get info on:

- how to land a date
- love advice
- anatomy 101
- how to break up with someone
- your love horoscope

Dialogue: María and Gustavo make a *cita*

Gustavo is into María. He decides to invite her out to dinner for their first *cita*, date...

GUSTAVO: **Hola María, es Gustavo.**

Hello, María, it's Gustavo.

MARÍA: **Hola Gustavito, ¿cómo estás?**

Hello, Gustavito, how are you?

GUSTAVO: **Bien, bien. Oye, qué vas a hacer este viernes?**

Good, good. Listen, what are you doing this Friday?

MARÍA: **Lo que tú quieras.**

Whatever you want.

GUSTAVO: **¡Qué bien! ¿Quieres salir a cenar?**

That's nice! Do you want to go out to dinner?

MARÍA: **Seguro, me encantaría.**

Sure, I'd love to.

GUSTAVO: **Maravilloso, te recojo a las siete.**

Great, I'll pick you up at 7.

MARÍA: **Vale, estaré lista.**

OK, I'll be ready.

Word Bytes

la cita	date
hacer	do
me encanta	I love it
querer	want
recoger	pick up
salir	go out
vale	OK

⏸ All That Slang

Things you say when making a date…

¿Cuándo nos podemos ver?	When can we see each other?
Estoy desesperado ♂/desesperada ♀ por verte.	I want to see you desperately. *You might sound a bit psycho, so mind your tone.*
Espero tu llamada.	I'll wait for your call. *Hey! One can wish…*
Te llamo.	I'll call you.
Me encantaría, guapo ♂/guapa ♀.	I would love to, handsome/beautiful.
Nos vemos mañana.	We'll see each other tomorrow.
Nos vemos ahorita.	We'll see each other soon.
¿Qué vas a hacer este sábado?	What are you doing this Saturday?
¿Quieres salir?	Do you want to go out? *Get straight to the point.*
Déjate de rodeos, invítame a salir.	Stop beating around the bush, invite me out.
¿Quieres tener una noche de pasión?	Do you want to have a night of passion?
Seguro.	Of course.
Te recojo a las nueve.	I'll pick you up at 9.
Vale, estaré listo ♂/lista ♀.	OK, I'll be ready.
No puedo…	I can't…
Estoy ocupado ♂/ocupada ♀.	I'm busy.
Me tengo que lavar el pelo.	I have to wash my hair. *Nice excuse.*
¿Qué tal el domingo?	How about Sunday?
Me gusta tu sentido del humor.	I like your sense of humor.
Eres un manisuelto.	You are touching too much.
Te estás pegando demasiado.	You are getting too close.
Si me tocas una vez más, te parto la cara.	If you touch me one more time, I'll break your face.

Use It or Lose It!

Gustavo and María arranged another *cita*—but you must arrange their conversation.

_____	**Me encantaría.**
_____	**Tremendo, vale.**
_____	**¿Quieres salir este jueves?**
_____	**Bien, te recojo a las cinco.**
_____	**¿Qué tal el viernes?**
_____	**No puedo, voy a salir con mis amigas.**

¿Quieres salir este jueves?; Do you want to go out this Thursday?; No puedo, voy a salir con mis amigas. I can't, I'm going out with my friends.; ¿Qué tal el viernes?; How about Friday?; Me encantaría. I'd love to.; Bien, te recojo a las cinco. Good, I'll pick you up at 5.; Tremendo, vale. Awesome. OK.

🔊 Use these *piropos*, pick-up lines, at your own risk!

Te ves muy bien.
You look great.

Estás muy guapo♂/ guapa♀.
You look handsome/beautiful.

Estás preciosa♀.
You look gorgeous.

Estás bien bueno♂/ buena♀.
You're fine.
This one can go both ways; it can be naughty if you don't know the person, but is safe if you're dating.

Hola, te invito a un trago.
Hello, I'll buy you a drink.

Mami, a ti no te duele nada.
Girl nothing hurts.

¡Arroz! que carne hay.
Give me some rice, here is the meat.
This is literally treating someone like a piece of meat.

Tanta curva y yo sin frenos.
So many curves, and I don't have brakes.

Are you ready to date a hot Latino or Latina?

1. You have a date in two hours. You:
   a. take a bath, spray on some perfume—all in all, you are *bien acicalado*. You also take a minute to relax and, of course, you check yourself in the mirror before going out.
   b. take a quick shower and then grab something out of the closet; you have to be quick since you don't know where your date lives.
   c. watch some TV, (hey, you took a bath in the morning), then take a leisurely stroll to the bus stop. Your date will meet you at the restaurant.

2. When talking to your dates, you usually feel:
   a. *tranquilo* ♂ /*tranquila* ♀.
   b. *nervioso* ♂ /*nerviosa* ♀.
   c. *indiferente*—you know there is always going to be another date.

3. The *piropo* you often use is:
   a. *Qué bien te ves.*
   b. *Estás bien bueno* ♂ /*buena* ♀.
   c. *¡Arroz! que carne hay.*

4. When the date is about to end you:
   a. ask *¿Cuándo nos vemos?*, then slip him/her a kiss on the cheek.
   b. ask *¿Qué vas a hacer el viernes?*
   c. become a *manisuelto* ♂ /*manisuelta* ♀.

Mainly A's:
Congratulations—*estás listo* ♂ /*lista* ♀.

Mainly B's:
You might be ready, but you need more practice.

Mainly C's:
Reschedule. Your manners and attitude need a lot of work before you attempt to date a Latino or Latina!

Q&A

Querida Paquita:
    What can I do to have a successful *cita* with a Spanish speaker?

    Manu

Querido Manu:
    Acicálate, tranquilízate, practica piropos, bromea, no seas manisuelto y llama. In a nutshell that is all you need to do: be clean, smell nice, relax, flirt, joke, don't touch too much and call back.

    Paquita

◀)Word Bytes

In order to have a successful love life, an anatomy lesson is essential.

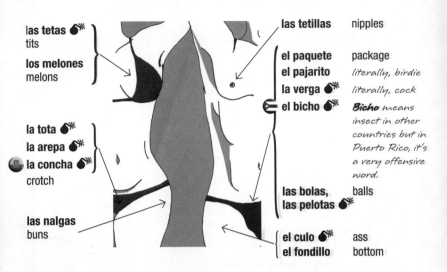

las tetas ●※
tits

los melones
melons

la tota ●※
la arepa ●※
🔵 **la concha** ●※
crotch

las nalgas
buns

las tetillas   nipples

el paquete   package
el pajarito   *literally, birdie*
la verga ●※   *literally, cock*
el bicho ●※   ***Bicho*** *means insect in other countries but in Puerto Rico, it's a very offensive word.*

las bolas,   balls
las pelotas ●※

el culo ●※   ass
el fondillo   bottom

Use It or Lose It!

You've gotta know your body parts. Go ahead and ID 'em.

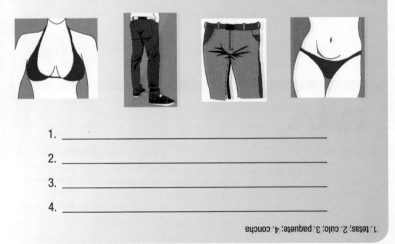

1. _____

2. _____

3. _____

4. _____

1. tetas; 2. culo; 3. paquete; 4. concha

🔊 All That Slang

Terms for foreplay…

besarse	kiss
besuquearse	kiss all over
grajearse	French kiss
sobarse	rub
desnudarse	get undressed

All about sex…

tener sexo	to have sex
acostarse	to sleep together
hacer el amor	to make love
hacerlo	to do it
se le paró	it went up
librarla	stop being a virgin

Other sex actions…

mamar	to suck
acabar/venirse	to finish/to come

Going solo…

tocarse	to touch oneself
hacerse una paja	to masturbate *this literally means to make hay*
hacerse una manuela	hand job *a bit of word play using the term **mano**, hand*

Positions…

el misionero/ la posición misionera	missionary
el perrito	doggy style
la tijera	scissors *one alternative, search the Kama Sutra for info…*
por atrás	back door *meaning from behind*

Though the terms below are most frequently used in the countries listed, they're understood by all Spanish speakers!

follar 🔴💥💥	to fuck
coger 〰️💥💥	to fuck *Note that **coger** is a verb that also means to take or grab.*
echar un polvo 💥💥	to ejaculate *literally, to throw dust* You may also hear this phrase in certain parts of Spanish-speaking South America and the Caribbean.

Gestures

💣✳ Banged somebody lately? Were you the one banged? With this fist move, everyone will understand.

💣✳ Push your tongue to your cheek then move it around; *sexo oral*, oral sex, is the intention. It's as sleazy as it sounds.

💣✳ Sometimes, saying OK with your fingers can mimic a body part: the ass. Although, most people know you are saying OK. Yet if you put your finger through the OK sign, you'll infer *por atrás*, anal sex.

💣✳ A caress with your finger on somebody's palm is an open invitation *a hacerlo*.

Use It or Lose It!

Try this fun game of foreplay—in Spanish—with your significant other(s). You'll need a dice and the guide below. Each player rolls the die, says the action aloud in Spanish, then acts it out. Repeat at your leisure. Have fun!

1. **toca a tu pareja**   touch your partner
2. **pierde un turno**   lose a turn
3. **tócate**   touch yourself
4. **besuquea**   kiss your partner all over
5. **recibe besuqueo**   get kissed
6. **lame**   lick

Una serenata

Word Bytes

el amor	love
el corazón	heart
largarse	get out *(said in anger)*
el odio	hate

Know-it-all/Sabelotodo

Being **cursi**, means being too cliché, that is, overly romantic and sappy to a fault. For example a **serenata** (serenade) is **cursi**. Sometimes being **cursi** works, sometimes it doesn't. It all depends on you or whom you're dating. Some people like sappy love, some don't.

Use It or Lose It!

Fela needs your help to deliver these lines in the correct order. What should she say first, next and last to get rid of Santiago? She also forgot some words, so you'll have to fill in some blanks.

¿Por qué no te _____?

Te _____, Santiago.

¡Qué _____!

 All That Slang

Talking about *amor* (or getting out of it) is sometimes difficult, especially if you don't know the language. Here are some good-to-know phrases.

Te amo.	I love you.
Te quiero.	*There is no exact translation for this one. Think of it as love for family, or use it when you're not quite ready to say I love you.*
Me interesas.	I'm interested in you.
Te deseo.	I want you.
Te odio.	I hate you.
¡Lárgate!	Leave!
No eres tú, soy yo.	It's not you, it's me.
¡Desgraciado ♂/Desgraciada♀!	Jerk!
¡Qué baboso ♂/babosa♀!	What a drooler! *Meaning a person who's boring as hell and/or drools a lot when kissing.*

What kind of a relationship are you in—or want?

Somos amigos con beneficios.	We're friends with benefits.
Somos amiguitos.	We're dating. *Not a serious couple yet...*
Estamos saliendo.	We're going out.
Somos novios.	We're boyfriend and girlfriend.
Somos amantes.	We're lovers.
El es su marinovio.	He is her live-in boyfriend. ***Marinovio*** *is a play between the word* ***marido***, *husband, and the word* ***novio***, *boyfriend.*

Use It or Lose It!

Can you guess the status of these relationships? Write 'em down—in Spanish.

1. Gary and Elena are dating frequently.

2. Leticia and Ramón are boyfriend and girlfriend.

3. Aida and Jorge *follan* occasionally.

4. Carlos lives with Julia.

1. Están saliendo; 2. Son novios; 3. Son amigos con beneficios; 4. Es su marido/novio.

Quiz

Are you a Latino♂/Latina♀ lover? Find out.

1. If your date says he likes you because you have a lot of meat on your bones, you shout ____ before storming out.
   a. ¡Desgraciado!
   b. Te quiero.
   c. Te odio.
   d. A and C

2. If you want to tell your partner you really love him/her, say:
   a. Te amo.
   b. Te quiero.
   c. Te odio.
   d. A and B

3. If you want to break up with someone, exclaim:
   a. Lárgate.
   b. Follar.
   c. Te odio.
   d. Te quiero.

4. Librarla means:
   a. Stop being a virgin.
   b. Be a sex addict.
   c. Be liberal.
   d. B and C

5. You are cursi if you:
   a. give your partner an awesome gift on your anniversary.
   b. design a postcard using glitter and send it to your date with a singing telegram.
   c. Take your date to a fancy restaurant.
   d. Open the door for your date.

1. d; 2. d; 3. a; 4. a; 5. b

Tu horóscopo

Will you be lucky in love? See what the stars say. In case you get lost:

- Keywords are in bold in both languages.
- *Número de la suerte* = lucky number.
- There is a visual guide to colors that complement you.

Aries

♈

Disfruta tu **viaje** y conocerás a un extrajero especial. No comentes sobre el **culo** de la persona en el avión.

Enjoy your **trip** and you will meet a special foreigner. Do not comment on the **ass** of the person on your flight.

Color: gris (gray)

Número de la suerte: siete (7)

Tauro

♉

Te gusta **hacerlo** como un toro, pero tu **pareja** actual prefiere que seas más **cursi**. Si eres virgen, es un buen momento para **librarla**.

You like **doing it** like a bull, but your present **partner** likes it a bit **sweeter**. This is a good time to **lose (your virginity)**.

Color: rojo pasión (passion red)

Número de la suerte: cinco (5)

Géminis

♊

Vas a conocer a unos **gemelos**, pero no tendrás suerte para hacer un **trío**. Invita a esa persona que te gusta a **salir**.

You will meet **twins**, but won't be lucky having a **threesome**. Invite the person you like to **go on a date**.

Color: beige (beige)

Número de la suerte: dos (2)

Cáncer

♋

No debes tener **una aventura**, te van a coger.

You shouldn't have **an affair**, you will get caught.

Color: verde (green)

Número de la suerte: uno (1)

Leo

♌

No vayas al zoológico, conocerás a **un amante feroz**.

Don't go to the zoo, you will meet **a fierce lover**.

Color: amarillo (yellow)

Número de la suerte: diez (10)

Virgo

♍

Deja a tu **amiguito**♂**/amiguita**♀. Es hora de **librarla**.

Leave your **"friend"**. It is time to **lose it (your virginity)**.

Color: violeta (purple)

Número de la suerte: dos (2)

Libra

♎

Trata nuevas **posiciones** en **la cama**.

Try new **positions** in **bed**.

Color: rosa (pink)

Número de la suerte: siete (7)

Escorpio

♏

Te van a **pellizcar** el **culo**. Disfruta.

Someone will **pinch** your **ass**. Enjoy.

Color: naranja (orange)

Número de la suerte: nueve (9)

Sagitario

♐

No tendrás suerte en el **amor**, tendrás que trabajar mucho.

You won't be lucky in **love**; you'll have to work too much.

Color: negro (black)

Número de la suerte: cero (0)

Capricornio

♑

Te las van a **pegar**. Tu amante te va a **dejar**. Vas a **conocer** a alguien.

Someone will **cheat** on you. Your lover will **leave** you. You will **meet** someone.

Color: azul marino (marine blue)

Número de la suerte: cuatro (4)

Acuario

♒

No es recomendable **hacerlo** en el agua.

It's not recommended that you **do it** under water.

Color: marrón (brown)

Número de la suerte: ocho (8)

Picis

♓

Cuando estés en una **cita** ordena el pescado, pero no olvides lavarte los dientes después o no te van a **besar**.

If you go out on a **date**, order the fish, but don't forget to wash your mouth or no one will **kiss** you.

Color: azul como el agua (aqua)

Número de la suerte: diez (10)

Use It or Lose It!

What is your best astrological match?

1. Who could join you for a great seafood dinner?

   a. **Pices**
   b. **Acuario**

2. If you want to start a new relationship with someone who has lots of free time, whom do you choose?

   a. **Sagitario**
   b. **Leo**

3. If you are peaceful, and want a high-energy *amante*, who is your best match?

   a. **Libra**
   b. **Escorpio**

4. Who should be together?

   a. **Virgo y Tauro**
   b. **Aries y Escorpio**

1. a; 2. b; 3. a; 4. a

Use It or Lose It!

What are their signs—in Spanish?

1. Mandy lacks any experience.

2. Andrés has the energy of a bull.

3. Lina's best color is marine blue.

1. Virgo; 2. Tauro; 3. Capricornio.

Internet

Get info on:

- using the internet in Spanish
- chatting, instant messaging and blogging
- social networking sites like Facebook® and MySpace®

🔊 Tech love

1
Vaya Alicia, ¿qué tal? Encontré un sitio web súper guay. Te envié el enlace y la contraseña.

2
¡Nítido! Estoy conectada y voy a chequear mi cuenta de correo electrónico.

3
Tema: ¿Viernes en la noche?
De: tipo_cool21@htbx.com
A: tecnochica20@htbx.com
Hola, vi tu perfil en HTBXAMOR. Me encantaría conocerte. ¿Quieres cenar conmigo el viernes en la noche? Envíame un correo electrónico, o vamos a hablar en línea. Haz click en el enlace para chatear.

4
¡Me respondio al correo electronico! ¡Voy a chatear ahora mismo!

5
¡Alicia, conseguí una cita!

6
¡Yo también!

7
Es hoy a las siete. En Le Rest.

8
¿¿Qué?! ¿ Tú eres tipo_cool21@htbx.com?

---

1 Hey Alicia, what's up? I found a super cool website. I forwarded the link and the password. **2** Cool! I'm connected and I'm checking my email.
3 Subject: Friday night? From: nice_guy21@htbx.com To: techgirl20@htbx.com Hi, I saw your profile on HTBXAMOR and I'd love to meet you. Can we have dinner on Friday night? Send me an email, or let's chat online. Click on the link to chat. **4** He wrote back! I'm going to chat right now!
5 Alicia, I've got a date! **6** Me too! **7** It's today at 7. At Le Rest. **8** What!? You're tipo_cool21@htbx.com?

Use It or Lose It!

Match the pics with their labels.

hacer click   contraseña   Estoy conectada.
Chequear tu cuenta de correo electrónico.

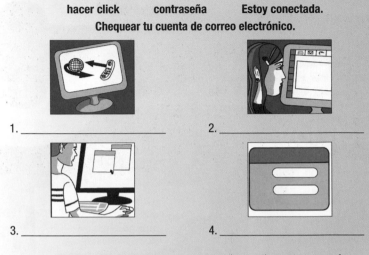

1._____   2._____

3._____   4._____

1. Estoy conectada. ; 2. Chequear tu cuenta de correo electrónico. ; 3. hacer click ; 4. contraseña

Know-it-all/Sabelotodo

Did you know that there is no one way of saying webpage in Spanish? You may see:

el lugar web   *el portal*   *el website*
la página web   *el sitio web*

Word Bytes

borrar	delete
el enlace	link
haz click	click
contestar	reply
el correo electrónico	e-mail
de	from
la dirección	address
enviar	to send

estar conectado al Internet	to be connected to the internet
hablar en línea/chatear	to chat *Hablar en línea is the pc term; chatear is the most popular term, though it's not proper Spanish.*
imprimir	print
el sitio web	website

All That Slang

More internet-savvy lingo…

¿Cuál es el enlace?	What's the link?
¿Estás seguro que quieres cancelar?	Are you sure you want to quit?
¿Quieres cerrar la sesión?	Do you want to log out?
Ella textea hasta que le duelan los dedos.	She texts until her fingers hurt.
Eugenio es un hacker.	Eugenio is a hacker.
Gonzalo descarga música pirata.	Gonzalo makes illegal music downloads.
Haz una búsqueda en Google™.	Search Google™.
Me gusta navegar la red.	I like surfing the net.
Mi servicio de Internet es una porquería.	My internet service sucks.
Necesitas abilitar las galletas.	You need to enable cookies.
Necesitas subir un programa.	You need to download a program.
No encuentro señal inalámbrica.	I can't get a wireless signal.
Puedes comprar eso en-línea.	You can buy that online.
Soy un internauta.	I'm an internet surfer.
Te chateo en la noche.	I'll chat with you tonight.
¿Cuál es tu contraseña?	What is your password? *Another term for* **contraseña** *is* **clave de acceso.**
Haz click en ese botón.	Click on that button.

Use It or Lose It!

Camil is confused—she wants to talk with Guido about an e-mail she received but she doesn't know the right words. Help her choose the correct words.

imprimir	correo electrónico	envió
dirección	portal	borré

Quiero _____ un _____ que Marta me
      (print)   (e-mail)

_____. El correo tiene la _____ de un
   (sent)   (address)

_____ bien nítido, pero creo que lo _____ …
   (website)   (erased)

imprimir; correo electrónico; envió; dirección; sitio web; borré

1. If you want to *acceder tu cuenta de correo electrónico*, you write your:
   a. *contraseña*
   b. *enlace*
   c. *cuenta*

2. If you surf the net frequently (as much as you blink), then someone might call you:
   a. *astronauta*
   b. *Internauta*
   c. *nerdo*

3. What's another way to say *contraseña*?
   a. *contrabando*
   b. *chateo*
   c. *clave de aceso*

4. What does it mean to *buscar* on the net?
   a. search
   b. cancel
   c. close

1. a; 2. b although some might call you c; 3. c; 4. a

Dialogue: Sonia & Manuel

Listen in on Sonia and Manuel, who are having an everyday conversation.

¿Hola?	Hello?
Hola, Sonia, es Manuel, ¿Cómo estás?	Hello, Sonia, it's Manuel, how are you?
Mi amor, te acabo de enviar un correo electrónico.	My love, I just sent you an e-mail.

MANUEL:	No una cadena, espero...	Not a chain, I hope...
SONIA:	No, no, es un enlace de Skype™ para poder chatear.	No, no, it's a link to Skype™, so we can chat.
MANUEL:	Bueno, pero prefiero usar el móvil.	OK, but I prefer to use the cell.
SONIA:	Tú siempre tan arcaico... Abre tu correo.	You're always so old-fashioned... Open your email.
MANUEL:	¡Ya está!	Done!
SONIA:	Bien, haz click en el enlace y así podemos chatear.	Good, click on the link and that way we can chat.
MANUEL:	Vale, te dejo.	OK, bye.
SONIA:	Chao.	Bye.

Dialogue: Sonia & Manuel text

After using the *enlace*, Sonia and Manuel begin to text.

SONIA:	Manu t veo...
MANUEL:	Q bien, tambien podemos hablar pr tel y video.
SONIA:	:)
MANUEL:	T llmo ahora.
SONIA:	Vale.

Manu I see you...

Good, this way we can also talk and have a video conference.

:)

I'll call you right now.

OK.

All That Slang

If you want to *chatear* or understand the *mensajes del boletín* (postings), follow this guide.

bn = bien	good
q = que	that, what, how
xq = por qué/porque	why/because
pto = punto	point, period
x = por	for or why
+ = más	more
– = menos	less
pdo = puedo	I can

tqm = Te quiero mucho.
I love you, I care for you.

muaks = beso
kiss *Muaks is what a kiss sounds like.*

GAD = Gracias a Dios
thank God

cm stas? = ¿Cómo estás?
how RU?

+ o – = más o menos
so, so

t odio = Te odio.
I hate you.

kbrn = cabrón 💣💣
asshole

TVS BN SXY = Te ves bien sexy.
You look very sexy.

xq no vienes esta noche? = ¿Por qué no vienes esta noche?
Why don't you come tonight?

t dseo = Te deseo.
I want you.

Know-it-all/Sabelotodo

Texting in Spanish doesn't involve too many abbreviations, but the beginning question and exclamation marks (¿ & ¡) are often cut and accents erased. Of course, words or syllables that sound like a letter are almost always replaced, like **t** for **te** and **c** for **ce**, and sometimes the vowels are cut out altogether.

Use It or Lose It!

What the heck do these texts say, in full Spanish? Read 'em out loud and figure 'em out!

Jorge:
Q kbrn eres.
cdtm,
Clau :P

Bebe:
¡Q bn t ves!
muaks

cdt
tqm
q cool rs

Jorge: Qué cabrón eres. Cuídate mucho, Clau = Jorge, you are such an ass. Take care, Clau.

Bebe: ¡Qué bien te ves! ¡Un beso! = You look great! A kiss for you!

cuídate = take care te quiero mucho = I care about you a lot que cool eres =you are very cool

Social networking en español

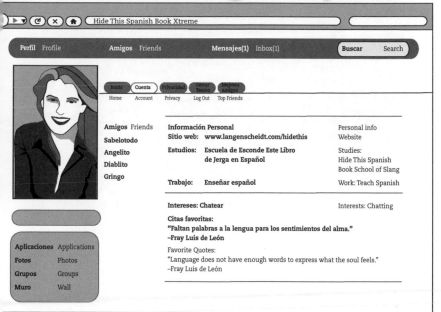

Perfil Profile   Amigos Friends   Mensajes(1) Inbox(1)   Buscar Search

Inicio | Cuenta | Privacidad | Cerrar Sesión | Mejores amigos
Home | Account | Privacy | Log Out | Top Friends

Amigos Friends
Sabelotodo
Angelito
Diablito
Gringo

Información Personal
Sitio web: www.langenscheidt.com/hidethis

Estudios: Escuela de Esconde Este Libro
             de Jerga en Español

Trabajo: Enseñar español

Intereses: Chatear

Citas favoritas:
"Faltan palabras a la lengua para los sentimientos del alma."
–Fray Luis de León

Personal info
Website

Studies:
Hide This Spanish
Book School of Slang

Work: Teach Spanish

Interests: Chatting

Favorite Quotes:
"Language does not have enough words to express what the soul feels."
–Fray Luis de León

Aplicaciones Applications
Fotos   Photos
Grupos   Groups
Muro   Wall

Hide This Spanish Book Xtreme

Use It or Lose It!

Can you remember three Spanish words on the Facebook® page that are similar in English?

What does **perfil** mean?

What does **inicio** mean?

What are your **intereses** and what is your **trabajo**?

Word Bytes

las aplicaciones	applications	**los intereses**	interests
buscar	search	**los mejores amigos/las mejores amigas**	bff
cerrar la sesión	close session		
la cuenta	account		
estudios	studies	**los mensajes**	messages
las fotos	photos	**el perfil**	profile
los grupos	groups	**la privacidad**	privacy
el inicio	start/home	**el trabajo**	work

Querida Paquita:

Do people from Spanish-speaking countries use specific social networking sites? I want to meet friends from Spain, Colombia, Honduras, Puerto Rico, etc.

Saludos,
Perfil

Querida Perfil:

Redes sociales, social networking websites, are definitely cool all over the Spanish-speaking world. Most Spanish speakers use—you guessed it—MySpace® and Facebook®. But, yes, there are *redes sociales* in Spanish, such as Buho21 and Quepasa.

Some things you can do to give your profile Hispanic flair is to change the language to Spanish and join a language or country-specific MySpace® or Facebook® group. You can also ask your friends to hook you up with Spanish-speaking friends—perhaps you'll find that there truly are just six degrees of separation (or maybe fewer).

Un abrazo,
Paquita

Online Dating

1 I'm going to search Gumersindo, my blind date for today. **2** BLOG: The sexiest man in South America, José César Chávez, Manuel Castro, Boberto Figueroa, GUMERSINDO M. Wikipedia, Entry: GUMERSINDO M., born in 1987. Bloggers, search for GUMERSINDO on the web..., You must blog to live. Blogging GUMERSINDO is the best, Blogging is the best, Meet GUMERSINDO, the sexy **3** WOW! Oh... he's here! **4** Hello, Desiré, I'm Gumersindo.

Word Bytes

bloguear	to blog	**las búsquedas**	searches
los blogueros	bloggers	**leer blogs**	to blog/to read blogs

You're not gonna find these blogging terms in a Spanish dictionary!

Know-it-all/Sabelotodo

When typing or texting in Spanish, accented letters may be replaced by empty boxes or strange symbols. That means the site you are using does not support the accented letters. To solve the problem, just leave out the accents. People will understand.

Use It or Lose It!

Connect the phrases at your highest speed.

1. to blog
2. blogger
3. to read blogs
4. blogging is the best

a. **bloguero**
b. **leer blogs**
c. **bloguear**
d. **bloguear es lo mejor**

1. c; 2. a; 3. b; 4. d

◑ All That Slang

Do you YouTube™? Go ahead—in Spanish.

Tienes que ver este video en YouTube™.	Check out this YouTube™ video. *Yep, that's right—Spanish speakers use YouTube™!*
¿Tienes una cuenta en YouTube™?	Do you have a YouTube™ account?
Los videos que se están viendo ahora…	Videos being watched right now…
¿Cómo puedo cargar un video?	How do I upload a video?
Ese video está brutal. Dale cinco estrellas.	That video rocks. Give it a five-star rating.
Ese video es una porquería. Dale una estrella.	That video sucks. Give it a one-star rating.
Comparte ese video.	Share that video.
¿Quieres hacer un comentario?	Would you like to comment?

Word Bytes

Buscar todos los videos	Search all videos
Buscar videos reproducibles en Google™	Search videos playable on Google™
Los más populares en blogs	Most blogged
Los más compartidos	Most shared
Los más vistos	Most viewed
Líderes	Movers & Shakers
Videos recomendados	Recommended videos
Explorar más videos	Explore more videos

Use It or Lose It!

Choose the correct phrase to answer each question.

1. If you want to tell your friend she must see an awesome video you say:
   a. **Tienes que ver este video en YouTube™.**
   b. **Los videos que se están viendo ahora.**

2. If you want to ask your newest friend if he has a YouTube™ account ask:
   a. **¿Cómo puedo cargar un video?**
   b. **¿Tienes una cuenta en YouTube™?**

3. If you want to pass good judgment on a video you say:
   a. **Ese video está brutal. Dale cinco estrellas.**
   b. **Ese video es una porquería. Dale una estrella.**

4. If you want to pass bad judgement on a video you say:
   a. **Ese video está brutal. Dale cinco estrellas.**
   b. **Ese video es una porquería. Dale una estrella.**

5. If a video is too cool to keep to yourself, say:
   a. **Comparte ese video.**
   b. **¿Quieres hacer un comentario?**

1. a; 2. b; 3. a; 4. b; 5. a

Know-it-all/Sabelotodo

Though YouTube's™ interface is in English, you can specify your country content preference by clicking on "Worldwide" and then on "Spain", "Mexico", etc. So, as you search on YouTube™, you'll see what videos Spanish speakers from your selected country are watching right now, their favorite videos, etc. Many of the videos selected will be in Spanish, so you'll have the added bonus of getting immediate access to contemporary Spanish language and visuals.

Google Video™ does interface in Spanish; go to video.google.es to immerse yourself in the Spanish world of online videos.

A-List

Cool and helpful websites for the tech-savvy Spanish speaker…

www.rae.es
  Spanish dictionary with verb conjugation
  feature from *Real Academia Española*

www.wordreference.com
  Bilingual dictionary with user forums to
  discuss words, slang, etc.

www.notesfromspain.com
  Spanish culture forum, from slang to fashion

www.terra.es
  Spanish search engine

www.videojuegos.com and
www.juegos.com
  Games in English and Spanish

www.esmascompras.com
  Shop in Spanish

www.redkaraoke.com
  Karaoke *en línea* (online)—it's free!

www.favoritosweb.com and
www.puntk.com
  The yellow pages of the internet

 Know-it-all/Sabelotodo

When searching online, try mx.yahoo.com (Yahoo!® Mexico),
es.yahoo.com (Yahoo!® Spain), telemundo.yahoo.com
(Yahoo for a variety of Spanish-speaking countries), or
www.google.com/intl/es (Google® in Spanish).

You can also change your computer's default language
from English to Spanish. This can usually be done
through the Preferences feature. If you wish to go back
to English, look for **Preferencias>Lenguajes** (sometimes
Idiomas)>**Inglés**.

Mixed Up

Who hasn't had an embarrassing e-mail mix up like Marina? Fill in the Spanish
terms to find out what happens…

a. term for webpage
b. place

c. body part
d. adjective

e. person (relation)
f. one word text message

Marina was checking her _____ at the _____. Suddenly, she
                                a   b

fell and *hizo click* on the wrong keys. Her entire contact list received a nasty message

along with a picture of her _____. In a few minutes, many people
                                    c

answered. Most of them were _____, including her _____,
                                        d   e

who said _____.
                f

Quiz

Are you internet savvy, ¿en español?

1. How many *perfiles* do you have?
    a. I have two, my left and my right.
    b. I have two, but I mostly use one.
    c. Three that I use and three that I don't.

2. *Un virus* is:
    a. a reason to miss a day of school or work.
    b. why you avoid *mensajes en cadenas*.
    c. the work of hackers (maybe your own)!

3. Your *servicio de Internet* is:
    a. something the phone company charges me for.
    b. DSL.
    c. *inalámbrico de alta velocidad* (cable).

4. RAM is:
    a. an uncastrated male sheep.
    b. something you like to upgrade to keep more stuff on your computer.
    c. Random Access Memory or, in Spanish, *memoria de acceso aleatorio o directo.*

5. *Una galleta* is:
    a. something delicious.
    b. something your computer stores.
    c. maintenance and tracking systems used by HTPS.

6. You use your *cuenta de correo electrónico:*
    a. once a week.
    b. for work and some jokes, daily.
    c. every five seconds.

Mainly A's
You still don't get what all the fuss is about the internet (boy, are you missing out)…

Mainly B's
You are a well-rounded internet user.

Mainly C's
You are an expert, *un nerdo♂/nerda♀ de computadoras.*

Gadgets

chapter 6

Get info on:

- names for trendy gadgets
- talking about your cool electronic stuff
- working your cell phone and MP3 player in Spanish

🔊 E-junk

1 ¡Lo logré! ¡ Inventé la e-Swiss Army Knife!

2 ¿Qué? Sí claro…

3 Mira, tiene teléfono móvil, con buzón de voz, mensaje de textos, Bluetooth™, reproductor de video y DVD, reproductor de música digital, cámara digital, correo electrónico, computadora con teclado y ratón…

4 Ramón, eso es lo mismo que un iPhone ® o una Blackberry ®, pero gigante e inconveniente.

5 Pero el mío imprime… y solo usa 20 baterías AA.

1 I made it! I invented the e-Swiss Army Knife! **2** What? Yeah right… **3** Look, it has a cell phone with voice mail, text messaging, Bluetooth™, video and DVD player, MP3 player, digital camera, e-mail, keyboard and mouse… **4** Ramón, that is the same thing as an iPhone® or a Blackberry®, but gigantic and inconvenient. **5** But mine prints… and it uses only 20 AA batteries.

◉ Word Bytes

la computadora *most used term*
el computador *used in some South American countries*
● **el ordenador**

computer

el teclado keyboard

computadora portátil
laptop
*You can also say **laptop**
with a Spanish accent.*

el ratón
mouse

la impresora
printer

el reproductor de vídeo, DVD y Blu-ray
video, DVD and Blu-ray player

*You could get away with just saying
vídeo, **DVD** (deh beh deh) or **Blu-ray**,
for example, **Enciende el DVD** (Turn on
the DVD).*

**la cámara digital
de fotos**
digital camera
*Of course, you
can just say
la cámara.*

**el teléfono
celular**
● **el móvil**
cell phone
*It's OK to
shorten
it to, simply,
celular.*

los audífonos
headphones

**el reproductor de música digital
el toca MP3**
MP3 player

las bocinas
speakers

la consola de juegos
Wii™, Playstation®, Xbox™, etc.
*Remember that you can
change these **consolas** to
Spanish!*

los videojuegos
video games

KEY: ● Spain

Use It or Lose It!

Can you find these gadgets in this *sopa de letras*?

1. consola
2. computadora
3. ordenador
4. ratón
5. móvil
6. audífonos
7. impresora
8. videojueos

```
T Ó N V I D E O J U E O S Í F O N Y
C O N S O L A Í D E O J U O R E R M
A D O Í F O N C O M P U T A D O R A
M P U R A T Ó N M P U M Ó E N A Y Ó
L A A U D Í F O N O S L A D O A H K
E N A M Ó O R D E N A D O R D E N L
O R D E N Í D M Ó V I L T Ó N M P U
A E O J U I Í F O N M P R E S O R A
```

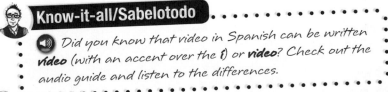

Q&A

Querida Paquita:
Are there Spanish terms for gadgets like the iPod®?
Saludos, Tita

Querida Tita:
Many of the gadgets out there retain their English name in Spanish. There is one difference, though—the pronunciation of the word.

ENGLISH/SPANISH GADGET	SPANISH PRONUNCIATION
PDA	peh deh ah
iPod®	eeh pohd
iPhone®	eeh fohn
MP3	eh-meh peh trehs
Blackberry®	Just like in English, but emphasize the double r
Palm Pilot®	pahlm pih-loht

I hope this guide helped you.
Paquita

Know-it-all/Sabelotodo

Did you know that video in Spanish can be written **vídeo** *(with an accent over the i) or* **video**? *Check out the audio guide and listen to the differences.*

◀Dialogue: When Gadgets Go Wrong

Hugo calls Raiza to talk about a cool gadget, but the reception is bad.
Let's see how Raiza reacts.

HUGO: **Aló, con Raiza, por favor.**
Hello, (can I speak) with Raiza, please.

RAIZA: **Sí hola, dígame pronto, la señal no está muy buena.**
Yes, hello, let me make this quick, the signal is bad.

HUGO: **Hola Raiza, ¿qué tal?**
Hello Raiza, how's it going?

RAIZA: **Bueno, ¿va a hablar?**
Well, are you going to say something?

HUGO: **Sí Raiza, es Hugo. Te quiero enseñar el nuevo el nuevo móvil que querías con cámara, video e Internet integrado.**
Yes, Raiza, it is Hugo. I want to show you the new cell you wanted with camera, video and integrated internet.

RAIZA: **Hola, hola, no te escucho, se está cortando.**
Hello, hello, I can't hear you, you're breaking up.

HUGO: **Coño Raiza, te estoy hablando.**
Damn it, Raiza, I'm talking to you.

HUGO: (to himself) **Este Bluetooth™ es una porquería.**
(to himself) This Bluetooth™ sucks.

RAIZA: **¡Ja! Cuando escuches el "bip", deja un mensaje.**
Ha! Leave a message after the beep.

CONTESTADOR: **BIP**
BEEP

HUGO: **Raiza, búscame en Skype™, tan pronto puedas, Y por favor, cambia el MALDITO mensaje en tu contestador...**
Raiza please, look me up on Skype™ ASAP; and please change this DAMN message...

Use It or Lose It!

Can you pass the polygraph? Write *verdadero* if the sentence is true or *falso* if it's false.

1. Raiza answered the phone, but the connection was bad.
2. "Leave a message after the beep" is *Cuando escuches el "bip", deja un mensaje.*
3. Hugo wants to show Raiza the latest and coolest phone, the one she wanted.

1. falso, Raiza never answered the phone, it was her voicemail message; 2. verdadero; 3. verdadero.

Word Bytes

For your cell phone…

pantalla — screen

menu — menu

teclado numérico — key pad

tecla — key

atrás	back	**números marcados**	dialed calls
ajustes	settings	**salir**	end/exit
altavoz	speaker phone	**silenciar microfono**	mute
enviar	send	**silencioso**	silent
llamadas recibidas	received calls	**sonar**	ring
llamar	call	**tono**	tone
nombres	contacts	**vibrar**	vibrate

Know-it-all/Sabelotodo

To change your phone to Spanish go to: menu> settings>phone>phone language>**Español**. Now, to change your phone back to English go to: **menú> configuración>teléfono>idioma del teléfono**>English. (Tabs and options may vary by phone.)

To send a text message go to: **Menú>mensajes>crear mensaje>enviar**.

Quiz What should you do to…

1. send a text message to your BFF from your *móvil*? Click:
   a. *menú>mensajes>crear mensaje*
   b. *menú>mensajes>buzón de mensajes*

2. call your friend Graciela? Go to:
   a. *nombres>Graciela>llamar*
   b. *nombres>Graciela>opciones*

3. turn your phone from ring to vibrate? Click:
   a. *resumen de llamada>salir>seleccionar*
   b. *ajustes>tonos>vibrar*

1. a; 2. a; 3. b

Word Bytes

For you MP3 player…

adelantar	forward
menú	menu
pausa	pause
reversa	back
rueda tactil/rueda de click	click wheel
selección	menu button
tocar	play
volumen	volume

ajustes de video	video settings	**cronómetro**	stopwatch
ajustes	settings	**fotos**	pictures, photos
álbumes	albums	**géneros**	genres
aleatorio	shuffle	**juegos**	games
aleatorio de canciones	shuffle songs	**listas rep.**	playlists
artistas	artists	**música**	music
audiolibros	audiobooks	**notas**	notes
autores	authors	**películas**	movies
bloqueo	block	**podcasts**	podcasts
búsqueda	search	**podcasts con video**	video podcast
calendario	calendar	**programas de TV**	TV shows
canciones	songs	**reloj**	clock
compositores	composers	**video**	video
contactos	contacts	**video clips**	music videos

Know-it-all/Sabelotodo

*Turn your MP3 player to Spanish. Just go to settings>language>**Español**. To turn it back to English go to **ajustes**>**idiomas**>English.*

�))All That Slang

Gadgets are great, except when they stop working… Here are a few lines you might need when technology works, or when it fails.

Se averió/jodió ✹✹ la computadora.
The computer broke/is fucked-up.

Tengo que llevar la computadora a un nerdo/reparación técnica.
I have to take the computer to a geek/ tech support.

La computadora tiene un virus.
The computer has a virus.

No me gusta el teclado ergonómico ni el ratón inalámbrico.
I don't like the ergonomic keyboard and wireless mouse.

Se me dañó el móvil.
My cell is damaged.

El teléfono no tiene servicio en esta área.
The phone has no service in this area.

Tengo pocas barras.
I have barely any bars.

Tengo que recargar la batería del teléfono.
I need to recharge the phone's battery.

Maldición✹, me se descargó el teléfono.
Damn it, the battery is dead.

Lo siento, se cortó la llamada.
I'm sorry, I lost the signal.

Ella ignoró mi llamada.
She ignored my phone call.

La llamada fue directo al buzón de voz.
The call went straight to voicemail.

Necesito escuchar mis mensajes de voz tan pronto como pueda.
I need to check my voicemail ASAP.

Déjame ponerte en altavoz.
Let me put you on speakerphone.

Ése teléfono es un dinosaurio.
That phone is a dinosaur.

Me prestas tu celular? Necesito hacer una llamada.
Can I borrow your cell? I need to make a call.

Déjame enviar este correo electrónico desde mi móvil.
Let me send this e-mail from my cell.

Tengo que reiniciar la iPod®.
I have to reset the iPod®.

Tengo que sincronizar la iPod®.
I have to sync the iPod®.

La iPod® está atorada.
The iPod® is frozen.

Descargué esa canción a mi computadora.
I downloaded that song to my computer.

¡Odio esta porquería/mierda de celular! ✹
I hate this crappy/shitty cell!

La cabrona computadora no funciona. ✹✹
The fucking computer isn't working.

Quiz Are you a gadget freak?

1. Your favorite electronic device is:
   a. you can't choose—you couldn't live without any of them.
   b. you can't decide between your *móvil*, your iPod® or your *computadora*.
   c. your *microondas* (microwave).

2. Your *móvil* is:
   a. a Blackberry® or an iPhone®—you need to be *conectado* at all times.
   b. a cool one with *cámara* and *video integrado*.
   c. standard issue—it came free with the contract.

3. You keep your *calendario*:
   a. on your Blackberry®, otherwise you couldn't function.
   b. on your computer's e-calendar.
   c. hanging on your wall...duh. You got it from Mom last year.

4. Your *música* listening schedule is:
   a. 24/7. You're always *conectado* to your iPod®, your *móvil* or your *computadora*.
   b. occasional. You like to do your chores while listening to your iPod®.
      Plus, you listen to CDs in the car.
   c. infrequent. You have some *bocinas*, speakers, at home that you connect
      to a *toca CD*.

Mainly A's
You are a child of the digital age. You are in, in technology. You may forget
that there is a whole (physical) world outside of your computer room...

Mainly B's
You are a well-balanced *chico♂/chica♀*. You use your gadgets to your advantage, but you still need someone to help you fix them when they fail.

Mainly C's
You must have been born in the dark ages. Why not take advantage of the
digital age and get tech savvy?

Write a list of spicy Spanish words you've picked up so far. Then insert them in
the text. What happens to Rafael?

a. name of gadget   b. noun   c. infinitive verb   d. place

Rafael broke his _____(b)_____ and decided to fix it using his _____(a)_____. Of

course it didn't work. Rafael decided he would instead _____(c)_____ the thing. That

didn't work either. "What can I do now?" he thought. Maybe he would just take the thing

to a _____(d)_____.

Style

Get info on:

- Latino fashion
- decorating your space—Latin style

🔊 The Dressing Room

Chica…No me gustan esos pantalones, se te ve la alcancía…Pero ¡el escote de esa blusa te queda fantástico!
Girl…I don't like those pants, your coin slot is showing…But the cleavage on that blouse is great on you!

¿Te gusta este bañador o éste?
Do you like this bathing suit or this one?

El entero, para nada. Mija, ¡con ese cuerpo necesitas el bikini!
The one-piece, no way. Girl, with that body, you need the bikini!

Vaya, ¡qué guapo te ves con ese traje! Pero necesitas una camisilla.
Wow, you look so handsome in that tux! But you need an undershirt.

Necesitas otro sostén y bragas para ese atuendo. Se te marcan...
You need a different bra and panties with that outfit. They're showing...

¡Ni sueñes que vas a salir con esas fachas!
Don't even dream of going out looking like that!

Pero...pero, la camisa, las medias y el sombrero y la correa están brutales...
But...but, the shirt, the socks, the hat and the belt are awesome.

Word Bytes

los accesorios	accessories	el collar	necklace
el abrigo	coat	la correa, el cinturón	belt
la alcancía	piggy bank	la falda	skirt
	Used when someone's butt crack or cleavage is showing, because it looks like a coin slot.	los jeans	jeans *In Spain, that would be **vaqueros** and in Puerto Rico, **mahones**.*
el atuendo	outfit	las medias	socks
el bañador	bathing suit	los pantalones	pants
la blusa	blouse	el probador	dressing room
las botas	boots	el reloj	watch
la braga	panties	el sostén	bra
los calzoncillos	underpants	los tacones	high heels
la camisa	shirt	el traje	tux, suit *Traje can also mean **vestido**.*
la camiseta	T-shirt		
la camisilla	undershirt	el vestido	dress
la chaqueta	jacket	los zapatos	shoes

Use It or Lose It!

In what order do you put on your clothes (assuming you're NOT a superhero)? Put each list of clothes in the right order.

1. **camiseta, jersey, sostén**
2. **pantalones, calzoncillos, correa**
3. **camisilla, corbata, camisa, abrigo**

3. camisilla, camisa, corbata, abrigo
2. calzoncillos, pantalones, correa
1. sostén, camiseta, jersey

All That Slang

Me queda bien/fatal.	It looks good/ugly.
Esos pantalones son chic.	Those pants are chic.
Esa falda es sexy.	That skirt is sexy.
Esa camisa es elegante.	That shirt is elegant.
Esos zapatos son espantosos.	Those shoes are horrible.
Los vaqueros te quedan muy apretados.	The jeans are too tight on you.
El escote es muy grande.	There's too much cleavage.
La falda es muy corta, no te tapa las nalgas.	That skirt is too short; it doesn't cover your butt.
Esa blusa es transparente.	That blouse is see-through.
Estás enseñando los cueros.	You're showing too much skin.
¡Qué ridículo♂/ridícula♀!	He/She looks ridiculous!
¿Qué lleva?	What is she/he wearing?
¿Te has mirado en el espejo?	Did you look in the mirror?
Esa camisa no pega con ese pantalón.	That shirt doesn't go with those pants.
¿Qué estabas pensando?	What were you thinking?
Súbete los pantalones, se te ve la raja.	Pull up your pants, your crack is showing.
Tienes la tiendita/jaula abierta.	Your shop/cage is open. *Meaning, your fly is down.*

¿Por qué no te cambias el vestido?
Why don't you change your dress?

¡Ese vestido es hermoso!
That dress is beautiful!

¡Esos zapatos están espectaculares!
Those shoes are spectacular!

Ese vestido te queda puñetero. 💣*
That dress looks fucking bad.

¡Ese vestido está cabrón! 💣*
That dress is fucking great!

¡Pareces un vagabundo♂/ una vagabunda♀ con esas porquerías de zapatos!
You look like a bum with those crappy shoes!

Do you know what to wear in order to *verte espectacular*?

¿Qué te pones para...?
What do you wear to...?

1. *ir a una entrevista de trabajo* (a work interview)
  a. *vaqueros, camiseta, chaqueta*
  b. *blusa/camisa, pantalones*
  c. *un traje de diseñador* (really expensive)—you better get the job if you want to be able to pay for it

2. *ir a una fiesta de gala* (a gala)
  a. *vaqueros, camiseta*
  b. *traje, corbata*
  c. *un vestido largo con tacones de* Jimmy Choo

3. *ir a la disco* (a dance club)
  a. *camiseta, pantalones*
  b. *una mini, tacones*
  c. *un vestido a la* Sex and the City

4. *acampar* (go camping)
  a. *una chaqueta o un vestido*
  b. *pantalones cortos, camiseta*
  c. a brand new *atuendo*, everything name brand of course, designer hiking boots and expensive *gafas de sol*

5. *ir a un centro comercial* (the mall)
  a. *bañador, tacones*
  b. *mahones, camisa/blusa*
  c. *mahones de diseñador, blusa* with bling and *zapatos de tacón*

Mostly A's
You have no idea of what is appropriate. Still, you feel comfortable in your clothes.

Mostly B's
You dress well, but you are not going on the cover of a magazine any time soon.

Mostly C's
You really know your fashion! But be careful, you might over do it sometimes, not to mention the hole your dressing habits leaves in your pockets.

Use It or Lose It!

The paparazzi are working the Latin Xtreme Music Awards. You are the Fashion Police. What will you say about each artist? Choose from the expressions below. Extra! See if you can find the biggest fashion faux pas. Here's a hint: it isn't one of the artists.

a. Ese pantalón te queda grande.

b. Esos zapatos son espantosos, no pegan con el vestido.

c. ¡Qué ridícula!

d. ¿Te has mirado en el espejo?

e. La falda es muy corta, no te cubre las nalgas.

f. El escote es muy grande.

g. Estás enseñando los cueros.

Faux pas: Tell that photographer on the left, whose huge crack is visible:

¡Está enseñando la alcancía!

Hello, this is Trading Interiors. In this episode the García sisters have traded houses and re-designed them to their taste. Let's see what they think about their rooms. **2** I love what you have done with the apartment. The kitchen appliances are the newest models. I love everything! The furniture is comfortable. I love the color combination. **3** My style is eclectic and my inspiration was the beach. **4** It has a painting of your family and a mirror on the ceiling. **5** How tacky. I don't like it! **6** The bed is pretty.

Use It or Lose It!

Can you pass the polygraph? Write *verdadero* if it's true and *falso* if it's false.

1. Rubi hates her *sala*.
2. Alejandra adores her *cuarto*.
3. There is a *cuadro* in Rubi's room.
4. *Cocina* is the place where you cook.

1. falso; 2. falso; 3. verdadero; 4. verdadero

Word Bytes

Some items and phrases you might have seen on *Intercambio de Interiores*...

la almohada	pillow
el apartamento	apartment *In Spain, they are called **pisos**.*
el candelabro	chandelier
la casa	house
clásico	classic
la combinación de colores	color combination
el cuadro	painting
diseñar	design
el dormitorio	bedroom
ecléctico	eclectic
el espejo	mirror

el gusto	taste
la habitación	room *You'll also hear **cuarto** or **dormitorio**.*
el librero	bookcase
la mesa	table
minimalista	minimalist
moderno	modern
el mueble	furniture
¡Qué mal gusto!	How tacky!
la silla	chair
el sofá	sofa
las velas	candles

Use It or Lose It!

What's up with *el dormitorio de Alejandra*? ID each hideous item in Spanish.

1. bed
2. pillow
3. window
4. painting
5. mirror

1. cama; 2. almohada; 3. ventana; 4. cuadro; 5. espejo

After the do-it-yourself era, these are the top things in interior design.

enseres electrodomésticos en acero inoxidable o cromo	chrome or stainless steel appliances
topes de granito para la cocina	granite counter tops
shows de diseño del hogar en televisión	home decorating shows
refrigerador de vinos	wine fridge
diseño verde	green design

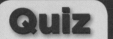

Quiz ¿Qué se vería mejor?

What would look better...?

1. in the red living room
  a. sofá *azul* with multicolored polka-dots
  b. sofá *marrón oscuro*

2. in the bedroom
  a. *una mesa*
  b. *una cama*

3. on an orange wall
  a. *un cuadro verde fosforescente*
  b. *un cuadro azul y blanco*

4. in the kitchen
  a. *cama de madera*
  b. *topes de granito*

Mostly A's: *Tienes mal gusto*
Please hire a designer; doing it yourself could be detrimental to your home.

Mostly B's: *Tienes buen gusto*
Are you a *diseñador*, a designer, or just naturally savvy with design?

amarillo	yellow	**gris**	gray	**rojo**	red
azul	blue	**marrón**	brown	**verde**	green
blanco	white	**negro**	black	**violeta**	purple

What do ya think of those colors? Put one of these after a color to describe it.

brillante, chillón (slang)	bright
fosforecente	hot (as in bright, e.g. hot pink)
oscuro	dark
pastel	pastel

Health

chapter 8

Get info on:

- relaxation: mind and body
- gross bodily functions
- STDs and other issues

All That Slang

Stressed out? Get it off your chest.

Tengo un mono trepado.	I have a monkey on my back. *Said when you have a neck spasm.*
Necesitas estirar tus músculos y relajarte.	You need to stretch your muscles and relax.
El trabajo y la uni/el cole me tienen loco♂/loca♀.	Work and college/school are driving me crazy. *La uni is short for university or college, and el cole is a private school from elementary to high school. If it's not private then it's called escuela.*
¿Quieres hacer yoga?	Do you want to do yoga?
No soy muy flexible.	I'm not very flexible.
¿Vamos al gimnasio?	Should we go to the gym?
¡No te preocupes, todo va a salir bien!	Don't worry, everything will be OK.
Uf, te ves muy tenso♂/tensa♀.	Wow, you look tense.
Relájate, sé feliz.	Relax, be happy.
Mi amor, ponte cómodo♂/cómoda♀, te voy a dar un masaje de pies a cabeza.	My love, get comfortable, I'm going to give you a head to toe massage.
Deberías relajarte, el estrés da arrugas.	You should relax, stress gives you wrinkles.

Use It or Lose It!

¡Relájate! Just follow this *ejercicio de relajación* and feel your tensions melt. For xtreme relaxation, see if you can follow the audio instructions without peeking at the book.

Busca una posición cómoda	Look for a comfortable position:
Siéntate o acuéstate y relájate.	Sit down or lay down, and relax.
Primero, respira profundo.	First, take a deep breath.
Inhala,	Inhale,
aguanta la respiración,	hold your breath
y exhala.	and exhale.
Tus hombros y el cuello ya no están tensos.	Your shoulders and neck are not tense.
Relaja tus ojos y boca.	Relax your eyes and mouth.
Eres feliz.	You are happy.
No dejes de respirar.	Don't stop breathing.
Ahora, levántate.	Now stand up.
Repite el ejercicio tres veces.	Repeat the exercise three times.

Use It or Lose It!

¿El estrés te está matando? Is stress killing you? These people are hurting too. Join each situation with the phrase that describes it.

1. Luigi has too much homework. He says…
2. Oli cannot reach his toes during yoga. He says…
3. Enid is stressing about everything. Your obligation as a friend is to warn her…
4. What you wish your boyfriend or girlfriend would say to you after a long day…
5. Dominic did not do the relaxation exercises for his *cuello*. Now he is complaining…
6. You notice your friend is too stressed. You suggest…

a. **Tengo un mono trepado.**
b. **La uni me tiene loco.**
c. **¿Quieres hacer yoga?**
d. **No soy muy flexible.**
e. **Déberías relajarte, el estrés da arrugas.**
f. **Mi amor, ponte cómodo♂/cómoda♀, te voy a dar un masaje de pies a cabeza.**

1. b; 2. d; 3. e; 4. f; 5. a; 6. c

All That Slang

Health isn't just about relaxation and stress. Here's the grosser side of taking care of your body.

Me estoy cagando/meando. 💣✳

I'm shitting/peeing myself.
Use this one when you really need a bathroom.

Estoy de carreritas. ¿Dónde está el baño?

I have the runs. Where's the bathroom?

¡Mierda, no hay papel! 💣✳

Shit, there's no TP!

¡Fo! ¿Quién fue el del pedo?

Yuck! Who farted?

Tengo la cara llena de granos.

My face is full of pimples.

Se me están saliendo los mocos.

I've got snot coming out of my nose.

Escupió tremendo gargajo.

He/She spit a big loogey.

Tengo tremendo catarrón.

I have a terrible cold.

Tamara vomitó hasta el verde de las tripas.

Tamara puked her guts out.
*Literally, **el verde de las tripas** means the green of the guts, the stuff that is supposed to be inside, never out.*

La borrachera de anoche me dejó con remenda resaca.

Last night's bender gave me a huge hangover.

Me duele la barriga/la espalda/la cabeza. Me siento miserable.

My tummy/back/head hurts. I feel miserable.

And for those special, below the belt, health situations:

¿Dónde están los anticonceptivos/ condones?

Where are the birth control pills/ condoms?

Ese ♂/Esa ♀ idiota me pegó los chancros.

That idiot gave me crabs.

Odio las enfermedades sexuales.

I hate STDs.
*The term for STDs is **ETS**, **enfermedades transmitidas sexualmente**.*

Know-it-all/Sabelotodo

When you say El está enfermo♂/Ella está enferma♀ you're saying that a person is sick. If you say El es un enfermo♂/ Ella es una enferma♀, you're saying that they are enfermos sexuales, which means that they're perverts.

When somebody sneezes, you should be polite and say *¡Salud!* (Health!) Can you figure out another situation when you'd say the same thing? Time's up... You also say *¡Salud!* as a toast.

Quiz What would you say when...?

1. you're out of TP:
  a. ¡Mierda, no hay papel!
  b. Nothing, you just use the receipt from your last purchase.
  c. ¡Me estoy cagando!

2. someone sneezes:
  a. ¡Salud!
  b. Cheers!
  c. ¡Mierda!

3. someone farts:
  a. ¡Fo! ¿Quien se tiró un pedo?
  b. What is that funky smell?
  c. Ese idiota me pegó los chancros.

4. your head aches, your body is producing excessive amounts of snot and you're coughing and sneezing like crazy:
  a. Tengo tremendo catarrón.
  b. I feel miserable.
  c. Eres un enfermo.

5. you make a pit stop at the pharmacy before an X-rated date:
  a. ¿Dónde están los anticonceptivos?
  b. Can I get a extra large condom?
  c. Tengo tremenda resaca.

Mainly A's
  Good for you, you really know your slang!

Mainly B's
  You really should try to speak more Spanish—you never know how much you've learned until you try it.

Mainly C's
  You have no idea what's going on around in any language. Careful! You might catch something nasty.

Go Green

chapter 9

Get info on:

- being green, Spanish style

Ser verde

All That Slang

Verde, green, lingo that you've gotta know...

¿Qué podemos hacer para mejorar el ambiente?	What can we do to improve the environment?
¿Me das un aventón en tu híbrido?	Can you give me a ride in your hybrid? *There is no Spanish word for carpool, so you can just say that you'll go together or that someone gives you **un aventón**.*
El ambiente está jodido.	The environment is fucked.
Hay mucho esmog.	There's a lot of smog.
Coño, qué calor, debe ser el efecto invernadero.	Damn it's hot; it must be the greenhouse effect.
¡Mierda! Se me olvidó traer la bolsa de tela.	Oh crap! I forgot to bring my own shopping bag.
Estela siempre lleva su termo de agua.	Estela always carries around her reusable water bottle.
David solo toma café en su taza termo.	David gets coffee only in his refillable travel mug.

Use It or Lose It!

Do you really know your *verde* lingo? Join the phrases to prove it.

a. **¿Qué podemos hacer para mejorar el ambiente?**

b. **¿Me das un aventón en tu híbrido?**

c. **El ambiente está jodido.**

d. **Hay mucho esmog.**

e. **Coño, qué calor, debe ser el efecto invernadero.**

f. **Ella siempre lleva su termo de agua.**

g. **¿Tienes taza termo?**

1. She always carries her reusable water bottle around.
2. The environment is fucked.
3. Can you give me a ride in your hybrid?
4. What can you do to improve the environment?
5. There is a lot of smog.
6. Damn, it is so hot, it must be the greenhouse effect.
7. Do you have a reusable travel mug?

a.4;b.3;c.2;d.5;e.1;f.6;g.1

1. At the end of a meal, you:
  a. wash the dishes by hand, with *jabón que no hace daño al ambiente* (eco-friendly soap).
  b. put the dishes in the dishwasher, but wait until it's full to turn it on.
  c. throw everything in the garbage, plates and all. Hey, that's what disposable plates are for!

2. When you go to *el supermercado* (the market) you:
  a. bring your own *bolsas*.
  b. request *bolsas de papel*, paper bags, and reuse them later.
  c. get paper bags in plastic bags. It's free, plus you wouldn't want anything to rip or break!

3. When you go on vacation, you:
  a. backpack or enjoy an ecotour—you want to be part of nature!
  b. make sure to turn off the lights and air conditioning in your hotel room when you leave for the day.
  c. live it up—there's no excess you can't handle!

4. You get around:
  a. by *bici* (bike) or *a pie* (by foot).
  b. *carro híbrido* (hybrid) or public transportation.
  c. SUV—you love that Hummer.

5. When you eat, you:
  a. use silverware, ceramic plates and cloth napkins, then you make a *composta* with the leftovers.
  b. use your own plates, but you always use paper napkins.
  c. use paper plates, and you double them so they don't leak.

6. You use your *aire acondicionado*:
  a. only if it's more than 100°F. You can handle heat waves with water, cold showers and maybe a fan while you are sleeping.
  b. for sleeping only. You go to the beach or the mall during the day to beat the heat.
  c. *todos los días*, every day! There's a reason why they exist, and you don't mind the electric bill.

Mainly A's: *Eres verde*
You are green as a tree in *primavera* (spring). If recycling were a religion, you would be the pope. Being green is good, just make sure you're not too smug about it.

Mainly B's: *Verde* in the making
You are trying to be green while maintaining some type of comfort. Keep working, it's worth it.

Mainly C's: *Eres un asesino de árboles*
Among other things, you are a "tree assassin". You better change your ways—the icebergs might just take it personally.

Travel

Get info on:

- must-see places
- the cash you need in Spanish-speaking countries
- hotel lingo
- bar and club lingo
- tasty treats and trendy drinks
- shopping

🔊 Las fotos de vacaciones

Yara is very forgetful and she's always misplacing things. For example, she just found an SD card from her digital camera with hundreds of pictures from various vacations. Now she's going through the photos and trying to figure out where she was and what she was doing.

Sí, recuerdo esto muy bien. Fui de crucero con mi familia. Tomé el sol en la piscina y, ¡me enfermé !
Oh, I remember this well. I went on a cruise with my family, I tanned out by the pool and I got sick!

Fui con mi hermana a Costa Rica y nos quedamos en un hotel boutique. Lo que más nos gustó fue ir a la playa todos los días. ¡La pasamos muy bien!
I went to Costa Rica with my sister and we stayed in a boutique hotel. What we enjoyed the most was going to the beach every day. It was so nice!

Adoro ir a los museos (aunque odio cuando hay tanta gente).
I adore going to museums (although I hate when there are so many people).

Fui a Ponce (en Puerto Rico) con mi novio, Tito. Paseamos por el centro del pueblo y nos perdimos. A Tito no le gusta pedir direcciones.
I went on a trip to Ponce (in Puerto Rico) with my boyfriend Tito. We went sightseeing around the town center, and got lost in the town. Tito doesn't like to ask for directions.

Fui de safari a la selva... pero los malditos animales no se dejaron ver.
I went on a safari in the jungle... but the damned animals didn't want to be seen.

Fui de mochilera por Europa. ¡Estuvo brutal! ¡Me fascina ir de aventuras!
I went backpacking in Europe. It was awesome! I love going on adventures!

Use It or Lose It!

Yara has finally posted all of her vacation pics to her blog and now she needs to add a description to each picture. Can you help her?

a.

b.

c.

d.

e.

f.

1. **Fui de safari a la selva.**

2. **Fui a pasear a Ponce con mi novio.**

3. **Fui de mochilera por Europa.**

4. **Hice un crucero con mi familia.**

5. **Fui al museo con mis amigos.**

6. **Me quedé en un hotel boutique con mi hermana.**

1. e; 2. d; 3. f; 4. a; 5. c; 6. b

 Are you a nice tourist or a naughty one?

ir a la playa, go to the beach	*ir a la playa nudista,* go to a nudist beach
get a *trago,* drink, in a local *barra*	get *borracho ♂/borracha ♀,* drunk, in a local *barra*
meet *alguien,* someone, at a club	go back to your hotel room with *alguien* you just met
ver una película, see a movie	*ver,* see, a peep show (which is just *peep show* in Spanish too!)
talk to a local in his or her language	insult a local in his or her language

A-List

Top 15 things to do in the Spanish-speaking world...

1. See Gaudí's *Sagrada Familia* Cathedral and *Casa Batlló* in Barcelona, Spain.
2. Kayak the bioluminescent pond in Fajardo, Puerto Rico.
3. Visit *Machu Picchu* ruins in Peru.
4. Climb *pirámides* in Mexico.
5. Drink *vino* (wine), *mate* (a bitter tea) and eat *churrasco* (skirt steak) in Argentina, while watching a tango show.
6. Enjoy *las Islas Galápagos*, an amazing wildlife reservation in Ecuador.
7. Snorkel in the Dominican Republic.
8. Catch the elusive *Aurora Austral* in the south of Argentina or Chile.
9. Eat a *tortilla española* (a Spanish egg and potato omelet) in Madrid, Spain.
10. Swim with the *delfines* (dolphins) and take a dive from the cliffs in Cancun, Mexico.
11. Hike the Andes.
12. See *Cruce de Bariloche*, a volcano in the clouds, which spans from Argentina to Chile.
13. Ride the *Amazonas* river in Peru, Venezuela, Colombia, Ecuador...
14. Participate in *la Tomatina*, the tomato throwing festival in Valencia, Spain. While you're there, eat *paella*.
15. See the toilet flush the other way anywhere beneath the equator.

Use It or Lose It!

Camille did the Xtreme vacation tour. Name the can't-miss experience in each picture from Camille's vacation album.

1. delfines
2. las Islas Galápagos
3. Pirámides Maya, México
4. tortilla española
5. Machu Picchu

◉Dialogue: El Sr. Trompa arrives at Hotel V

Hotel V is *un hotel boutique* in the imaginary city of Santa Juana. Check out its awesome amenities. Mr. Trompa, an annoying first time client, is checking in.

LINA:	**Bienvenido Sr. Trompa. Su habitación es la Warhol, con vista al mar.**	Welcome Mr. Trompa. Your room is the Warhol, with an ocean view.
SR. TROMPA:	**Gracias. Oye, Lina, ¿hay Internet inalámbrico en la habitación?**	Thanks. Hey, Lina, is there wireless internet in the room?
LINA:	**Sí en todo el hotel. También hay videojuegos y videos gratis.**	Yes, everywhere in the hotel. There are also free video games and videos.
SR. TROMPA:	**¿Qué otras amenidades hay?**	What other amenities are there?
LINA:	**Muchas; tenemos una barra, un restaurante de tapas y fusión asiática/latina, spa, piscina, centro de negocios, barra de jugos y meriendas complementarias, servicio de valet, estacionamiento para los huéspedes, alquiler de bicis y móviles, y muchas cositas más. Aquí tiene un folleto de información.**	We have a bar, a tapas restaurant with Asian/Latin fusion, spa, pool, business center, juice bar, complimentary snacks, valet service, parking for guests, bike and cell phone rental and a lot of other things. Here's a brochure with all the info.
SR. TROMPA:	**¿Y me puedo llevar los champús del hotel?**	And, can I take the hotel's shampoos?
LINA:	**Seguro.**	Of course.
SR. TROMPA:	**¡Vaya, qué hotel más guay!**	Wow, what a cool hotel!
SR. TROMPA:	**Por último, ¿en dónde queda el ascensor?**	One last thing, where's the elevator?
LINA:	**Uy, no hay...tiene que usar las escaleras.**	Uh-uh, there isn't one...you have to use the stairs.
SR. TROMPA:	**(to himself) ¿Qué coño es esto? ¿No hay un pinche ascensor?**	What the hell? There's no damn elevator?

Use It or Lose It!

The Hotel V quality department is keeping tabs on Lina to asses her service. Help them fill in the blanks in this phone call made from a *móvil* with poor reception.

LINA: Buenas tardes, Hotel V.

FRANCO: Hola, ¿hay Internet inalábrico en la _____ (room)?

LINA: Sí en _____ (everywhere in the hotel). También _____ (there are) videojuegos y videos _____ (free).

FRANCO: ¿Qué otras _____ (things) hay?

LINA: Muchas, tenemos una ____ (bar), un _____ (tapas restaurant), spa, _____ (pool), centro de negocios, barra de jugos, servicio de valet estacionamiento para los _____ (guests), alquiler de _____ (bikes) y móviles, y muchas cositas más.

FRANCO: ¡Vaya, qué _____ (hotel) más _____ (cool)!

habitación; todo el hotel; hay; gratis; cosas; barra; restaurante de tapas; piscina; huéspedes; bicis; hotel; guay

All That Slang

Travel light, travel right… But when it comes to naming your luggage in Spanish the same concept of less is more does not apply.

el equipaje	luggage
el equipaje de mano	carry-on luggage
el bolso	bag/purse/backpack
la bolsa	bag (as in paper or plastic)

How to say luggage when in…

la maleta

la petaca *Be careful, **petacas** also means butt cheeks!*

la valija *Note: South America and Central America use both **maleta** and **valija**.*

KEY: Cuba Dominican Republic Mexio Puerto Rico Spain

89

Use It or Lose It!

Everybody has some baggage, but what do they call it? Write the term for *equipaje* you'd be likely to hear in each place.

 Puerto Rico _____

Spain _____

Mexico _____

Colombia _____

Q&A

Querida Paquita:
    Instead of staying in a typical, boring hotel, I want to try something different on my next trip to Spain. What do you suggest?

Atentamente,
Confundido

Querido Confundido:
    Apart from hostels, *los intercambios de casas*, house swappings, are becoming more popular by the minute (think "The Holiday", the movie with Jude Law and Jack Black). Just do an online search to find an organization that'll put you in touch with other house swappers. You pay a small fee, which insures your home from damages, and you may need to sign a contract. House swapping is a great way to savor the local culture, and save some money on a long trip. Be sure to ask for plenty of pictures of the place and research the area and organization you select to work with.

Saludos,
Paquita

Querida Paquita:
    I'm a frenzied student who desperately needs a vacation. Which Spanish-speaking country can I visit last minute?

Yours,
Apurado

Querido Apurado:
    If you are in the US and don't have a passport, Puerto Rico is your only option, since it's a US commonwealth and requires just a government-issued picture ID for US citizens. If you do have a passport, add Mexico and the Dominican Republic to your list of possible last-minute destinations. Which to chose? Depends on where you live!

Saludos,
Paquita

When you travel you...

1. a. speak English to everybody—somebody is bound to understand you.
   b. learn some phrases in the country's language—especially the naughty ones!
   c. learn the language and memorize your Hide This Book Xtreme.

2. a. arrive with 20 *petacas* and then some. You never know what you are going to need.
   b. travel with three *maletas*, enough to last you a week and a half.
   c. travel with *equipage ligero* (light). You'll get what you need along the way.

3. a. ask if you can use *dólares*.
   b. exchange money at the airport and keep it in a safe place in your pants.
   c. exchange a bit of cash at the airport and keep your credit card handy.

4. a. stay at a hotel with a name in English—it's the only brand you trust.
   b. stay at a *hotel boutique* with the top amenities in case you hate the city.
   c. stay with friends family or in a hostel—you like to experience the city the way locals do.

5. a. take your most comfortable shoes, shorts and T-shirts; it's your vacation and you plan to dress like it.
   b. pack your most stylish clothing. You live by the saying: *A la moda aunque me joda* 💣※ (In fashion even if it fucks me up).
   c. know what the locals are wearing before you go. You don't want to stand out!

6. a. find the fast-food joints—you'll survive on burgers and fries.
   b. study the travel guides. They've gotta have the best advice, right?
   c. ask some locals you meet at a bar, your taxi driver and the clerk at your hotel for recommendations.

7. a. are constantly asked where you're from, even before you open your mouth.
   b. are asked where you're from after people talk to you.
   c. are asked directions by other *turistas*.

Mainly A's:
   You are the tourist of all tourists, and you're not embarrassed by it. That's OK—it helps you enjoy the city comfortably. Be careful, though: you might be taken advantage of if you're not alert.

Mainly B's:
   You try to blend in, but you won't fool anybody. Still, you get a true taste of your vacationing place, and locals appreciate when you make an effort.

Mainly C's:
   You can easily pass as a local, though you probably have your I'm-a-tourist-please-help-me moments.

◀ All That Slang

¡Qué día! What a day! So, what's the weather like while you're on your travels?

¿Cómo va a estar el tiempo?	What will the weather be like?
Va a llover/nevar/tronar/hacer calor.	It will rain/snow/thunder/be hot.
El día está como para mmm… 💣✳	It's a good day for having…sex. *Usually used when it's rainy.*
El día está perfecto.	The day is perfect.
Está lloviendo a cántaros.	It's raining cats and dogs. *Literally, it's raining jars.*
Hace un calor cabrón. 💣✳	It's fuckin' hot.
Hace un frío puñetero. 💣✳	It's fuckin' cold.
⬤ **¡Joder tío, qué calor!**	Damn it's hot, dude!

Know-it-all/Sabelotodo

Another common weather phrase is **Se están casando las brujas** *(The witches are getting married). This means it's raining but the sun is shining.*

Use It or Lose It!

Pair the pics with a caption from the word bank.

¡Joder tío, qué calor!
Está lloviendo a cántaros.

Se están casando las brujas.
Hace un frío puñetero.

1. It's raining cats and dogs.

2. Damn it's hot, dude!

3. It's fuckin' cold.

4. Sunshine and rain.

1. Está lloviendo a cántaros.; 2. ¡Joder tío, qué calor!; 3. Hace un frío puñetero.; 4. Se están casando las brujas.

◉ All That Slang

Now that you can talk about the local weather, learn how to talk about the local food.

Tengo antojo de tapas.	I'm in the mood for tapas.
Vamos a un restaurante in.	Let's go to an in restaurant.
¡Guácatela! Eso es muy grasoso.	Disgusting! That's too greasy.
¡Fo, qué asco!	Yuck, that's disgusting!
¡Mmm, qué delicioso!	Mmm, that's delicious!
¿Quiéres repetir?	Do you want seconds?
No gracias, estoy a dieta.	No thanks, I'm on a diet.
Come, estás muy flaco♂/flaca♀.	Eat, you're too skinny.
¿Por qué no aguantas el pico? Estás un poquito gordito♂/gordita♀.	Why don't you hold your beak? You're a bit chunky.
¡Buen provecho!	Enjoy your meal!
¡Uf! Estoy que exploto.	Oof! I'm about to explode.
¡Qué tremenda hartera!	I'm so full!
¡Me voy a morir del hambre!	I'm starving! *Literally, I'm dying of hunger!*
Que te caiga como te caigo yo.	I hope you choke on it. *Literally, I hope that you digest what you are eating as well as you digest me. OK, it doesn't translate well, but you can use this phrase instead of* **buen provecho** *with people who don't really like you, or as a joke.*

Use It or Lose It!

What do you say when:

1. …something is disgusting?
2. …something is good?
3. …you want your enemy to choke on it?
4. …you want someone to enjoy a meal?
5. …you don't want any more food because you're trying to lose weight?

1. ¡Fo!/¡Guácatela!; 2. Mmm, qué delicioso!; 3. ¡Que te caiga como te caigo yo!; 4. Buen provecho!; 5. No gracias, estoy a dieta.

A-List

Food you've gotta try…

1. **chapulines** from Mexico—cured grasshoppers covered in seasonings or chocolate (yes it says grasshoppers)

2. **arepas**—a toasty Venezuelan or Colombian corn patty; you can enjoy it with **pabellón,** stewed meat, ripe plantains and **frijoles** (beans)

3. anything made with **plátanos** (plantains)

4. a real **quesadilla**, with a thick, hand-made **tortilla** and fresh white cheese

5. **churrasco**, skirt steak, in **chimichurri** sauce, the Argentine version of pesto

6. **tortilla de patatas**—a potato omelet courtesy of Spain

7. **arroz**, rice—be it in **paella**, with **frijoles** (beans) or stewed with chicken

8. **tamales**—a corn patty, filled with meat or cheese, steamed on a corn husk (don't try eating the husk, it tastes like dirty paper)

9. **cachapa**—a sweet corn pancake

10.  **piragua,**  **nieve**—the tropical version of the snow cone

11. **helado de fruta natural**—all natural fruit ice

12. **flan**—the Latin version of custard or crème caramel

13. **dulce de leche**—if you think the ice cream is good, wait till you try the real thing

14. **quesito frito**—a fresh, fried cheese

15. **empanadas**—savory turnovers

Drinks you can't miss…

1. **tequila** or **mezcal**—the latter has the real worm, and is another powerful liquor made from the agave plant

2. **coquito**—the Caribbean coconut version of eggnog with rum and coconut milk, but no eggs

3. **agua de coco**—fresh coconut water

4. **anís antioqueño**—anise liquor from Colombia; it's very strong

5. **Cerveza Presidente**—a specialty beer from the Dominican Republic; if you're in Puerto Rico, try **Medalla**

6. **mojito** with **Ron Don Q Añejo** or **Consulado** (types of liquor)

7. **chicha**—a fermented rice drink (be careful to say **chicha** just in Venezuela and the surrounding countries; in the Caribbean **chicha** is the third person singular of **chichar**, a very, very vulgar way to say "to have sex")

8. **jugos de frutas**—if you're not looking to get **borracho,** drunk, try fresh **guayaba** (guava), **tamarindo** (tamarind) or **acerola** (Caribbean cherry) juice

9. **soda de piña**—pineapple soda

All That Slang

Get your groove on by talking about *clubs, barras* and *discos*.

Ese club es bueno.	That club is good.
Dan música variada: tecno/tropical/rock/reguetón.	They play different types of music: techno/tropical/rock/reggaeton.
Esta noche hay banda/evento.	There's a band/event tonight.
DJ Pepo toca esta noche.	DJ Pepo is spinning tonight.
El trago de esta noche es el martini de guayaba.	Tonight's drink is the guava martini.
Esta noche: cerveza a dos por una.	Tonight beer is 2 for 1.
Esta noche es noche de damas. Chicas entran gratis.	Tonight is ladies' night. Girls get in free.
El costo por entrada es de 10$.	The cover is $10.
No me gusta el ambiente.	I don't like the atmosphere.
El club cierra a las 2 a.m.	The club closes at 2 a.m.
	In Spanish, a.m. is pronounced "ah eh-meh".
¿Esta es la entrada de VIP?	Is this the VIP entrance?

Use It or Lose It!

Are you cool enough to know where each event happens?

a.

b.

c.

1. **Esta noche hay juego de fútbol.**
2. **Esta noche hay banda de rock.**
3. **Hoy es noche de damas.**

a. 2; b. 3; c. 1

Nice and naughty club speak...

¿Quieres bailar?
Do you want to dance?

Te invito a un trago.
I'll buy you a drink.

Es el club más pegaᵒ.
It's the *in* club.

Vamos a perrear. 💣✳
Let's grind.
Perrear *is a vulgar term that means dancing to **reguetón**. It's a small step up from actually getting it on on the dance floor.*

Mami, tienes que estar seca después de mover tanto ese culo.
Girl, you must be parched after all that ass shaking.

Es el club más cabrón. 💣✳
It's the best fucking club.

 Q&A

Querida Paquita:
How can I find a cool Latino club? Tito

Querido Tito:
The Latin world is full of party venues and drinking shacks. Use common sense when trying to find the best one. Try asking young locals: *¿Cuál es el mejor club?* Which is the best club? Hot spots change quickly—what was in today is not in tomorrow, but these additional guidelines will help you:
Check out the crowd, is the place full?
How's the music?
Do they have any good promotions like a special drink or ladies' night?
Who's playing?
Check the décor—if it's too tacky, run.
Sports bars tend to be good on *fútbol* (soccer) nights or special events. Otherwise you'll get stuck hanging out with old dudes who don't have cable.
If the cover is too expensive, you can be sure it's either very, very exclusive or it's tourist oriented. It might be good, but you won't get the local flavor. Paquita

Querida Paquita:
How old do I have to be to get into a bar in the Spanish-speaking world? Jorgito

Querido Jorgito:
You must be 18 to drink in most Spanish-speaking places, and some bars and clubs raise the age limit in order to attract a more exclusive crowd. Still, most places follow a don't ask, don't tell policy. Don't embarrass yourself, though, by trying to get in when you're underage. Paquita

◄)) All That Slang

If you want to travel you will need to exchange your dollars or pounds to *pesos* or *euros*. Here's a guide to what people really call their money in Spanish-speaking countries.

el euro
Some people still use the old Spanish terms **pesetas** and **duros**.

el peso cubano, peso convertible
There are two currencies in Cuba, and **cuc** is a nickname for 'em.

el boliviano
This is also called **peso**.

el peso chileno
Call it **el billullo**; if you're lucky enough to have a 500 bill, call it **la quina**.

el peso colombiano
They call it **el billete**.

el colón
aka **las lucas**

el colón costarricense
Las cañas are bills, and **el tucán** is 5000 **colones**.

el peso mexicano
You might hear **el pachuco**.

el sol
Some might say **la villega**.

el bolivar
The slang would be **los riales**.

el peso argentino
The slang term is **los mangos**.

el dólar americano
Call it **el billuzo** to get by on the streets.

el dólar americano
No one really says **dólares americanos**, they just say **pesos**.

Dinero is the official translation for money, but just like you would say someone has a lot of dough, Spanish also has slang terms for *dinero*. Here are a few. These all mean cash, although most have other meanings as well:

la lana
wool

la plata
silver

los cocos
coconuts *This is common in the Caribbean, and often used cynically:* **Te tendré que pagar con cocos.** *(I'll have to pay you in coconuts.)*

los chavos
This means cash in Puerto Rico, but kids in Mexico... Go figure.

el menudo
It's an old-school boy band, cow brains in Mexico, a derogatory adjective that means small or insignificant and slang for coins.

KEY: Argentina Bolivia Chile Colombia Costa Rica Cuba Ecuador
Mexico Peru Puerto Rico El Salvador Spain Venezuela

Use It or Lose It!

Explain the monetary misunderstanding in the comic below.

Dame tus chavos.
Give me your _____.

Pero, ¡es mi único hijo!
But, he's my only son!

Hint: fill in the blank to understand the joke.

Chavos means "money" in Puerto Rico, but "kids" in Mexico. The robber says "give me your money" but the woman thinks he means "give me your kids".

Dialogue: Sin chavos

Bobi and Belinda are in a restaurant; they just had dinner. When *la cuenta* comes, Bobi checks his wallet...

BOBI: Belinda, estoy en la prángana.	Belinda, I'm broke.
BELINDA: ¿Y yo que voy a hacer? Se me ha quedado la cartera. (annoyed)	And what am I going to do? I don't have my purse.
BOBI: No sé...	I don't know...
BELINDA: ¿Seguro que no tienes nada?	Are you sure you don't have anything?
BOBI: Ni un centavo.	Not a cent.
BELINDA: Eres un pela'o.	You're broke.
BOBI: ¡Qué lío! Vamos a tener que fregar los platos.	What a mess! We're going to have to do the dishes.
BELINDA: ¡Los platos! Los platos los friega tu abuela. Chao.	The dishes! Your grandma can clean the dishes. See ya.
BOBI: Pero... Belinda...Espera... Belinda!	But...Belinda...Wait...Belinda!

Word Bytes

fregar	clean (dishes)
pela'o	broke
los platos	dishes
la prángana	extreme poverty
tener	to have

All That Slang

Broke? It's OK to admit it…

Estoy pela'o.	I'm dried out.
Estoy en la prángana.	I'm broke.
No tengo ni un centavo.	I don't even have a penny.
El/Ella es pobre.	He/She is poor.

But if you have money…

Estás forra'o♂/forr'á♀.	You're loaded.
	This is a very common phrase in Puerto Rico.
Él/Ella es rico♂/rica♀.	He/she is rich.
La billetera está gorda.	The wallet is fat.

Gesture

Is your *pareja* (partner) cheap? Tap your elbow with an open hand twice, and everybody will get the picture.

Quiz Loaded or Empty

Can you accurately say if there is a lot or little cash flow?

1. You know that *estás pela'o* when:
   a. your wallet is full.
   b. your wallet is empty.

2. You know you've got some cash when:
   a. *la billetera está gorda.*
   b. *no tienes ni un centavo.*

3. You're *rico♂/rica♀* when friends say:
   a. *estás forra'o♂/forr'á♀.*
   b. *eres un pela'o.*

4. You gotta file for bankruptcy when:
   a. *eres rico♂/rica♀.*
   b. *estás en la prángana.*

1. b; 2. a; 3. a; 4. b

A-List

Now that you have the cash, get some souvenirs to remember your *viaje*. Avoid buying plastic magnets; here's a list of must-have souvenirs.

1. Spain: *un abanico de mano*, a hand fan that can range in price from 1 euro to 2,000 euros or more.
2. Argentina: *cuero* (leather)—you'll get great quality at pleather prices.
3. Mexico and Peru: *plata* (silver) jewelry
4. Cuba, Puerto Rico, Dominican Republic: *máscara de carnaval*, carnival mask
5. local music you can find only on your travels (no, you can't get it on iTunes®, so don't even bother)

Know-it-all/Sabelotodo

If you ever went to Spain and found yourself all alone in town in the middle of the day, you weren't in the twilight zone! Spaniards enjoy a midday **siesta**, nap (usually from 1–2 p.m.). Most stores close at that time and reopen later. Keep in mind that, in Spain, stores open at 10 a.m. and close between 5 and 7 p.m. And be sure not to leave your shopping for Sunday—most of the Spanish-speaking world believes in resting on Sunday.

◖All That Slang

Some useful phrases when you are *de compras* (shopping) and trying to get a good deal.

¿Cuánto cuesta?	How much does it cost?
¿Hay rebajas?	Are there sales?
	You might also see **ventas** *or* **especiales** *instead of* **rebajas**.
Me están timando.	They are ripping me off.
Le doy 10$ y quedamos.	I'll give you $10 and we're good.
Si me lo da por 5€, me lo llevo ahora mismo.	If you give it to me for 5€, I'll take it right now.
1$, es mi última oferta.	$1, it's my last offer.
Quédeselo, al cabo que ni me importa.	Keep it, I don't really care.
¿Cuánto me rebaja si compro dos?	How much less if I buy two?

Use It or Lose It!

Are you ready to bargain *en español*? Match the Spanish with the English equivalent.

1. **Me están timando.**
2. **1$, es mi última oferta.**
3. **Le doy 10$ y quedamos.**
4. **Quédeselo, al cabo que ni me importa.**
5. **Si me lo da por 5€, me lo llevo ahora mismo.**

a. I'll give you $10 and we're good.
b. They are ripping me off.
c. If you give it to me for 5€, I'll take it right now.
d. $1, it's my last offer.
e. Keep it, I don't really care.

1.b; 2.d; 3.a; 4.e; 5.c

Know-it-all/Sabelotodo

¿Dónde puedo comprar...? Where can I buy...? Don't know where to get the essentials? Here's a short guide.

- *la farmacia* — pharmacy
- *la ferretería* — hardware store
- *la joyería* — jewelry store
- *la librería* — book store
- *la tienda de calzado* — shoe store

Use It or Lose It!

Welcome to *Xtreme Centro Comercial*, the mall! On your last day of vacation you still have some *compras* (shopping) to do. With the list in hand, find the stores you need and write the name of the store next to the item. The first letter of the name of each store where you found the items will spell a secret word.

Lista de compras
- *unos aretes*
- *un CD*
- *una taza*
- *un cuadro*
- *un abanico de mano*
- *algo para el dolor de cabeza* (something for a headache)
- *un vestido*
- *un libro para el viaje*
- *unos audífonos* (headphones)
- *unas bragas sexy*

Where to buy: unos aretes = Vázquez e Hijos Joyería; un CD = Audio Tienda; una taza = Curiosidades Turísticas; un cuadro = Arte y Decoraciones; un abanico de mano = Curiosidades Turísticas; algo para el dolor de cabeza = Ibuprofén; un vestido = Orlando; un libro para el viaje = Nobles Librería; unos audífonos = Electro Hut; unas bragas sexy = Secretos; So what was your secret word? Vacaciones, vacation, of course!

la tienda de electrónicas	electronics store
la tienda de música	music store
la tienda de ropa de caballeros	men's clothing store
la tienda de ropa de mujer	women's clothing store
la tienda de ropa íntima	lingerie store
la tienda de ropa	clothing store
la zapatería	shoe repair

Free Time

Get info on:

- the hottest Spanish music
- film *en español*
- what's on TV
- Spanish magazines and newspapers

Música cool

ANTONIO:	**Hey Julisa, ¿qué haces?**	Hey Julisa, what are you doing?
JULISA:	**Aquí escuchando un poco de música.**	Just listening to a little music.
ANTONIO:	**¿Qué escuchas?**	What are you listening to?
JULISA:	**Reguetón, es mi género favorito.**	Reggaeton, it's my favorite kind.
ANTONIO:	**A mi también me gusta, pero prefiero el rock.**	I like it too, but I like rock better.
JULISA:	**Esta noche hay un concierto de Don Polaco, ¡vamos!**	There's a Don Polaco concert tonight, let's go!
ANTONIO:	**Vale, pero no conozco su música.**	OK, but I don't know the music.
JULISA:	**No importa, lo mejor es bailar. Aunque su lírica está brutal.**	It doesn't matter, the best part is dancing. But his lyrics are awesome.
ANTONIO:	**¿Mi hermana puede venir? A ella también le fascina el reguetón.**	Can my sister come? She loves reggaeton too.
JULISA:	**Seguro, yo invito a los demás chicos y así vamos en bonche.**	Sure, I'll invite the rest of the guys and we'll all go as a group.
ANTONIO:	**Listo. Entonces nos vemos esta noche.**	Cool. Then I'll see you tonight.

Use It or Lose It!

Can you pass the polygraph? Write *verdadero* if it's true and *falso* if it's not.

1. Antonio's favorite music is reggaeton.
2. Antonio and Julisa are going to a concert tonight.
3. A *bonche* is a group of friends.
4. Don Polaco's lyrics are great.
5. Don Polaco is a *reguetón* singer.

1. *falso.* Antonio prefers rock.; 2. *verdadero,* 3. *verdadero,* 4. *verdadero,*
5. *verdadero,* FYI *reguetón* artists are also called *raperos.*

Querida Paquita:
What is the *in* music genre right now in Spanish-speaking places?
Saludos,
Mike

Querido Mike:
Many people are listening to *reguetón,* also written *regateón* or reggaeton. It's a pretty new kind of music, a mix of rap, hip-hop and afro-Caribbean beats—basically a Latino kind of hip-hop. It's so popular that all the other genres, like *salsa, pop, merengue, baladas,* etc., usually include a collaboration with a *reguetón* artist. You probably don't want to play this for your Mom, though. The lyrics tend to be about fast cars and not-so-subtle references to sex.
People also really like *baladas-pop,* which is slow pop music, like ballads. *Rock* has gotten a little less popular, but in the end if you can dance to it and sing it, people will listen.
Saludos,
Paquita

Querida Paquita:
How do you dance *reguetón?*
Saludos,
Pies Izquierdo (Left Feet)

Querido Pies Izquierdo:
Reguetón is a lot like hip-hop and rap with a Latin twist, but the key to dancing it is to shake your ass! Move your butt in circles to the beat of the music, and don't forget to move your hips too. Then, if you're feeling confident, it's time to get low. Keep moving to the beat and go lower and lower. This is called the *hasta abajo* (all the way down) move, and people will probably chant that when they see you going down. When *reguetón* was first getting popular, this dancing was scandalous, because people said it was like "having sex with your clothes on". The moves are still the same but now everybody dances this way, and no one seems embarrassed.
Saludos,
Paquita

◉All That Slang

You need more entertainment than just music. Here's the slang on movies.

Esa película está pegá'.	That movie is a hit.
Esa película es…	That movie is…
…**comiquísima.**	…very funny.
…**muy triste.**	…very sad.
…**romantiquísima.**	…so romantic.
…**un éxito taquillero.**	…a blockbuster.
…**una porquería.**	…garbage.
Es una película rosita.	It's a chick flick.
	Literally, it's a pink movie.
¿Qué tipo de película es?	What type of movie is it?
Es…	It's…
…**comedia.**	…a comedy.
…**romance.**	…a romance.
…**drama.**	…a drama.
…**suspenso.**	…a suspense film.
…**horror/terror.**	…a horror/terror film.
…**acción.**	…an action film.
…**artes marciales.**	…a martial arts film.
Estoy loco♂/loca♀ por ver esa película.	I'm dying to see that movie.
	No need for a doctor! Just go see it.
No puedo ver películas sin palomitas de maíz y una soda.	I can't watch movies without popcorn and soda.
	Most people just say **popcorn** *instead of* **palomitas de maíz** *or* **palomitas**. *By the way* **palomitas** *are little doves…go figure.*
¿Por qué no te callas? 💣※	Why don't you shut up?
	For that jerk who won't let you enjoy the movie.

If you want to bring out your inner critic, here are a few things you can say about the flicks.

★	**Es una mierda. 💣※**	It's shit.
★★	**Regular, medio medio (medio buena y medio porquería).**	So, so.
★★★	**Buena.**	Good.
★★★★	**Un éxito, súper cool.**	A hit, super cool.

Use It or Lose It!

Bea is a first time critic on a radio show. She's so nervous, she doesn't know what to say. Help her get her words out, in Spanish. She thinks that:

1. The movie is a blockbuster but it is slow.

   _____

2. It's a chick flick, and it's funny.

   _____

3. The movie is shit.

   _____

4. There's another movie that she's dying to see.

   _____

1. La película está pegá', pero es lenta.; 2. Es una película rosita y comiquísima.; 3. Es una mierda. ; 4. Estoy loca por ver esa película.

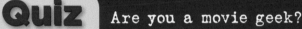

Quiz   Are you a movie geek?

1. When you go to the movies you buy:
   a. your *taquilla* (ticket), and nothing else. You don't like being distracted.
   b. *palomitas* and soda to munch while you enjoy the movie.
   c. *palomitas,* soda and chocolates. You spend the movie eating and throwing your snacks at people.

2. You get your *taquillas:*
   a. at least one hour before the movie starts.
   b. 15 to 30 minutes before it starts, so you get in after the commercials.
   c. as a distraction after an unsuccessful shopping day. It doesn't matter if the movie already started.

3. Your favorite time to go to the movies is:
   a. if it's a great movie, you'll be at the premiere, no matter what time it is.
   b. a weekend night. It's a good way to start a long weekend.
   c. never, you'd rather rent the DVD.

4. You agree with the *críticos de películas* (film critics):
   a. almost always, in fact, you send them recommendations.
   b. almost never, you loved all three Die Hards!
   c. ¿*Críticos?* You don't know and you don't care.

Mostly A's:
   The seats at your nearest *cinema* have an imprint of your butt. You might want to give it a break…or not.

Mostly B's:
   You like going to the movies, but you also like doing other things. Good for you.

Mostly C's:
   You couldn't care less about the movies! You've got better ways to spend your free time.

⦿All That Slang

TV lingo for couch potatoes…

Baja/sube el volumen.	Turn down/up the volume.
¿Van a dar algo bueno?	Are they showing anything good?
Lo único que están dando es basura.	There's nothing on.
¿Estás criando papas de nuevo?	Are you growing potatoes again?

The Hispanic version of being a couch potato.

Estoy adicta a este programa.	I'm addicted to this show.
Me perdí el episodio de anoche de Lost.	I missed last night's episode of Lost.
Cuéntame qué ha pasado.	Tell me what happened.
Ponme al día en la novela.	Catch me up on the soap.

Use It or Lose It!

What would you say if…

1. …you want to know if there will be anything good on TV?
2. …it's 2 a.m. and there are only infomercials on TV?
3. …you want to tell your friend that he's a couch potato?
4. …you're considering a 12-step plan for your addiction to soap operas?
5. …you're pissed for missing last Saturday's SNL episode?
6. …you need your friend to tell you what happened last week in the soap?
7. …you want your friend to tell you what happened?
8. …you can't hear a thing?
9. …your ears are about to explode?

a. **Lo único que están dando es basura.**
b. **Baja el volumen.**
c. **Estoy adicta a este programa.**
d. **¿Van a dar algo bueno?**
e. **Ponme al día en la novela.**
f. **Me perdí el episodio de anoche de SNL.**
g. **Cuéntame qué ha pasado.**
h. **¿Estás criando papas de nuevo?**
i. **Sube el volumen.**

1. d; 2. a; 3. h; 4. c; 5. f; 6. e; 7. g; 8. i; 9. b

A-List

Don't miss these online series.

Cálico electrónico

www.calicoelectronico.com

This flash series from Spain is highly offensive and funny! It's about a janitor who has multiple personalities, one of them an S&M super hero. Watch online for free weekly episodes or subscribe and pay to see back episodes.

Los huevos

www.huevocartoon.com

Huevocartoon.com is a community where eggs are the characters and comedy is their life. The site features two-minute clips starring Shakespearean eggs, mariachi eggs, gay eggs…you get the picture. The website is based in Mexico. You can watch some clips for free, buy a subscription or check out their channel on youtube.com. The Eggs became so popular that a movie was made featuring them.

Los güebones

www.guebones.com

A play on the insult *huevón* (to have big balls or to be a dummy), *Los güebones* make short clips to parody life in Spain. One of their most famous clips is *Ya peco por ti* (I Sin For You) where fictional fans send their problems to a priest, and he commits the sins for them so they don't have to ask for forgiveness later.

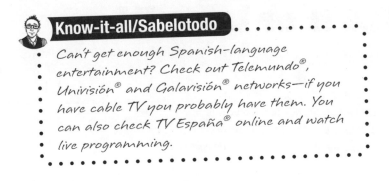

Know-it-all/Sabelotodo

Can't get enough Spanish-language entertainment? Check out Telemundo®, Univisión® and Galavisión® networks—if you have cable TV you probably have them. You can also check TV España® online and watch live programming.

All That Slang

Tu favorito... What would you rather do?

Ver una obra de teatro.	Watch a play.
Ir a un concierto.	Go to a concert.
Ir a la ópera.	Go to the opera.
Ver el ballet.	See the ballet.
Ir al circo.	Go to the circus.
Ver un musical.	Watch a musical.

Everybody's a critic. Talking about performances...

Es un performance experimental, nadie la entiende.	It is an experimental performance; nobody understands it.
Me dijeron que la obra de teatro estaba excelente/porquería.	They told me that the play was excellent/awful.
El musical estuvo aburrido/divertido.	The musical was boring/fun.
El coro cantó fantástico/fatal.	The choir sang wonderfully/terribly.
El bailarín ♂/La bailarina ♀ se cayó.	The ballerina fell.
Uf, fue demasiado largo.	Ugh, it was too long.

Use It or Lose It!

Can you pass the polygraph? Write *verdadero* if it's true and *falso* if it's not.

1. If the *bailarina* was good, she was *fatal*.
2. If *la obra estuvo aburrida*, then it was awesome.
3. You'd rather *ir a un concierto* than *ver el ballet*.
4. *El concierto* was good because it was *demasiado largo*.

1. *Falso*; she was *excelente*. *Fatal* means bad.
2. *Falso*; that means it was boring.
3. That is really up to you.
4. *Falso*; if the concert was good you wouldn't think it was *demasiado largo*; too long.

Word Bytes

los clásicos	classics
el/la comelibros	bookworm, literally a book-eater
equilibrado ♂ / equilibrada ♀	well-rounded
holgazán ♂ /holgazana ♀	slacker
	Another popular word is **vago** ♂ / **vaga** ♀.
el/la intelectual	intellectual
el libro	book
el periódico	newspaper
la revista	magazine
la tirilla cómica	comic strip

QUIZ What type of reader are you?

1. Lees (you read):
   a. todos los días (every day) for fun.
   b. todos los días so that you can keep up in class discussions.
   c. nunca (never).
   d. una o dos veces por semana (once or twice a week).

2. Your favorite genre is:
   a. todos (everything).
   b. history, philosophy and clásicos.
   c. tirillas cómicas (but only if you're forced to read something).
   d. revistas y novelas populares (bestsellers).

3. In a conversation about libros, you:
   a. don't really talk. That would mean you'd have to put your book down!
   b. dominate the conversation. You tend to lose control when talking about books.
   c. are completely bored out of your mind.
   d. can keep up, if you feel like it.

4. The last thing you read was:
   a. Gabriel García Márquez's Cien años de soledad (One Hundred Years of Solitude), some news articles, your Spanish textbook...
   b. all the top books from the New York Times book review.
   c. Don Quijote...Cliff Notes.
   d. a revista de modas (fashion magazine), el periódico and half a chapter of Isabel Allende's latest novela.

Mostly A's:
   You are a comelibros. You devour books like there is no tomorrow.

Mostly B's:
   You are an intelectual. You read a lot, and you let people know you do.

Mostly C's:
   You are a holgazán♂/holgazána♀. You hate reading (or anything that requires energy).

Mostly D's:
   You are equilibrado♂/equilibrada♀, a well-rounded reader.

Q&A

Querida Paquita:
   I'm a total comelibros, but I want the time I spend reading to be productive too. Is reading a good way to learn Spanish?
   Saludos, Lexy

Querida Lexy:
   Sure, why not?! Look for books with bilingual editions, or read the newspaper, magazines or a blog. If you want a break from books, you can watch TV shows like telenovelas or movies with subtitles in Spanish—that way you can listen and read.
   Saludos, Paquita

Bad Language

12

Get info on:

- cursing
- how to know you've been insulted
- how to fight back

DISCLAIMER

We don't recommend using these words and expressions but in case you overhear them, we want you to know what people are saying! We are not responsible if you get a black eye or a rearranged smile from using these insults. Warning! There are no 💣💣 in this chapter, because all the language is bad!

A-List: Top 10 *malas palabras*

mierda	shit
coño	*Literally, this means something like cunt, but it's a versatile curse word and can be used to express anger.*
pendejo	an asshole, dumb ass *Literally, hair in the ass*
Me vale madre.	I give a fuck. *This one sounds really funny in English—"I care a mother", but the meaning is much, much more vulgar.*
hijo♂/hija♀ de puta	son of a bitch
cagarse en…	to shit on… (something, someone or an idea) *You can add any word to the end, although the most common are **la leche** (milk) in Spain, and **diez** (10) because it sounds like **dios** (God). It's used just like damn, but it's harsher.*
joder	to fuck, to screw *Straightforward and simple.*
puñeta	jerk off *This is a big one. It may be used in anger, to express pain, disbelief, misfortune, misery, etc. It refers to male masturbation.*
cojones	balls *Say **¡Qué cojones!** when someone does something irrational or against you. Keep in mind that it does not imply courage as it does in English (i.e., to have the balls to do something).*
cabrón	motherfucker *This is the cream of the crop. Literally **cabrón** is a male goat, but the English equivalent is more like motherfucker.*

Use It or Lose It!

Meet Joe W., the biggest *pendejo*, asshole, ever. Look at the things people have said about him, and see if you can describe him in English. Write the translation next to the Spanish.

MEET JOE W.

1. He's **un hijo de puta**.

2. His favorite curse word is **joder**.

3. He is **un pendejo**.

4. He has big **cojones**.

5. He is full of **mierda**.

1. a son of a bitch
2. fuck
3. an asshole
4. balls
5. shit

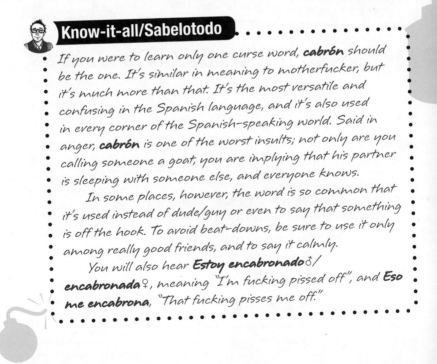

Know-it-all/Sabelotodo

If you were to learn only one curse word, **cabrón** should be the one. It's similar in meaning to motherfucker, but it's much more than that. It's the most versatile and confusing in the Spanish language, and it's also used in every corner of the Spanish-speaking world. Said in anger, **cabrón** is one of the worst insults; not only are you calling someone a goat, you are implying that his partner is sleeping with someone else, and everyone knows.

In some places, however, the word is so common that it's used instead of dude/guy or even to say that something is off the hook. To avoid beat-downs, be sure to use it only among really good friends, and to say it calmly.

You will also hear **Estoy encabronado**♂/**encabronada**♀, meaning "I'm fucking pissed off", and **Eso me encabrona**, "That fucking pisses me off."

Q&A

Querida Paquita,
My Spanish-speaking friends are major guttermouths, and I want to keep up. Are there any more nasty words I should know?
Yours,
Patty Mouz

Querida Patty:
These are the *malas palabras* that did not make the countdown...

carajo
It is used just like *coño*.

comemierda
Literally, shit-eater, this is a very common expression in the Caribbean for a stuck-up person.

puta
If you want to insult a "lady" and you are aiming for the jugular, go for this one. Basically it means bitch or whore.

puto
Male version of *puta*.

gilipollas
dick, jackass

mamao
Literally, this means the same as *pendejo*. It's mostly used in the Caribbean to mean sucker.

pinche
Use this to describe something or someone; it basically means damn or fuck. This adjective is courtesy of Mexico.

maldita sea/maldición
A classic damn or damn it.

Paquita

Use It or Lose It!

Fill in the correct usage of *cabrón* for each picture.

a. ¡Estoy encabronada!

b. ¿Cómo estás, cabrón?

c. ¡Eres un cabrón!

d. ¡Eso está cabrón!

1.

2.

3.

4. FREE for all people with red T-shirts!

¡GRATIS para todas las personas con camisetas rojas!

KEY: 1.c; 2.a; 3.b; 4.d

Use It or Lose It!

What did that potty mouth just say? Complete the naughty expressions.

a. **Eres un** _____.

b. **Me** _____**en tu madre.**

c. **Estoy muy molesto; estoy** _____.

d. **Eres un idiota; eres un** _____.

e. **¡**_____**! ¡Qué dolor**
_____ **tengo!**

a. cabrón/pendejo; b. cago; c. encabronado/encojonado; d. mamao/pendejo; e. Coño/Carajo, hijo de puta

¿Las señoritas educadas no deben decir malas palabras?

Polite ladies shouldn't curse?

¡Coño! ¡Carajo!
¡Puñeta! ¡Me cago en diez!
Shit! Damn it!
Jack off! Shit!

¡Auch!
Ouch!

Use It or Lose It!

Can you remember what these words mean?

a. **¡Coño!**
b. **¡Carajo!**
c. **¡Puñeta!**
d. **¡Me cago en diez!**

Gentle ways to express anger and the not-so-gentle...

Me caso en diez.
Literally, I marry in ten.

The switcharoo of **cago** *with* **caso***, and* **dios** *with* **diez***, makes this senseless phrase work.*

Me importa un pepino.
I don't care.

Literally, I don't give a pickle.

¡Qué pantalones!
What nerve!

Literally, What pants!

¡Qué chavienda!
Fudge!

¡No me jorobes!
Don't bother me!

Me cago en tu madre.
I shit on your mother.

Me importa tres carajos.
I don't give a fuck.

¡Qué cojones!
What balls!

¡Qué jodienda!
Fuck!

¡No me jodas!
Don't fuck with me!

Use It or Lose It!

Write the PG substitute for each curse word.

1. Me **cago en tu madre**.
2. Me importa **tres carajos**.
3. ¡Qué **cojones**!
4. ¡Qué **jodienda**!
5. ¡No me **jodas**!

Quiz How dirty are you?

For each situation, choose one way of responding. You will get points depending on how you respond—the dirtier, the better.

1. Your just received your paper on how to make the world *verde*. You got a crappy score with a frowning face (your teacher has a childish sense of humor). Meanwhile, your best friends are very excited because they all got high marks (and a smiley), and one of them comes over to tell you. You say:
   a. *Me importa un pepino.*
   b. *Me importa tres carajos.*

2. Someone just cut you off while you were driving. He gives you the finger, and you almost hit another car. You scream:
   a. *¡Qué pantalones!*
   b. *¡Qué cojones!*

3. You've been dying for a double hot fudge brownie sundae with extra cherries. When you finally get it, the *nerdo* kid working the counter trips and throws it on your white T-shirt. You shout:
   a. *Me cago en tu madre.*
   b. *Me caso en diez.*

4. You just spotted a huge zit on the tip of your nose. You say to yourself:
   a. *¡Qué chavienda!*
   b. *¡Qué jodienda!*

5. Your best friend is bothering you about an ugly shirt you wore to a party last night.
   a. *¡No me jodas!*
   b. *¡No me jorobes!*

If you had 9 points or fewer, you are a bit of a goody two-shoes. Work on your dark side; you never know when you might need it.

If you had 10 or more points you are just mean! Congratulations, you have a very good extended vocabulary.

5: a=3 points; b=2 points
4: a=1 point; b=3 points
3: a=5 points; b=2 points
2: a=1 point; b=3 points
1: a=1 point; b=2 points

⏴All That Slang

A course in curse… Learn the proper ways to be improper.

¡Maldita sea mi suerte!

Damn my luck!

Me cago en la mierda.

I shit in the shit.

*Redundancies and hyperbole are always good resources for cursing in Spanish. You can substitute **la mierda** for **la leche** (milk), **'na** (nothing), **diez** (10) or, really, anything.*

¿Qué crees, que me estaba haciendo una puñeta♂/soplando la pájara♀?

What do you think I was doing, jacking off?

Use this when someone accuses you of procrastinating, for example, if your boss sends you half way around town for his coffee and then says "I've been waiting for you" when you finally get back.

¡Qué jodienda!
¡Joder!

Fuck!

¡Jódete!

Fuck you!

Estoy jodido.

I'm fucked.

¡Coño, por qué no recoges ese reguero!

Damn it, why don't you pick up this mess!

El Señor Smith es un hijo de puta.

Mr. Smith is a son of a bitch.

El concierto estuvo hijoeputa.

The concert was fuckin' awesome.

El partido de fútbol estuvo cabrón.

The soccer game was fucking great.

Cabrón, ése fue el mejor partido de fútbol.

Dude, that was the best soccer game.

¡Qué cojonudo eres!

You have some balls!

Laura no quizo venir porque tiene un barrito, ¡qué pendeja!

Laura didn't want to come because she has a zit. What a dumbass!

¡Vete al carajo!/¡Vete a la mierda!

Go to hell!

Perdimos el pinche/cabrón partido.

We lost the damn game.

Me encojona que diga eso.

It fucking pisses me off when he/she says that.

¡Puta madre!

Literally, Whore mother!

This expresses misfortune, anger, pain, amazement, etc.

¡Qué comemierda esa María! Estuvo hablando toda la noche de su ropa de marca.

María is a shit-eater! She spent the whole night talking about her designer clothing.

Eres un gilipollas.

You're a dick.

Use It or Lose It!

Carlitos received this *correo electrónico* from his friend Dale, but he left out all the curses! Can you help him turn this into an R-rated email?

Hey _____ (dude) 💣※

i_____! (whore mother) The soccer game was _____ (fucking awesome). _____ (It fucking pisses me off) that we lost. i_____! (fuck) Laura didn't come 'cause she had a zit. I told her _____ (go to the shit) and she got pissed off at me. Whatever, _____ (I don't give a fuck).

See you later, _____ (dude) 💣※

Dale

🔊Dialogue: The interview

Susan is a reporter for the network Unimundo. Her first assignment is to interview Paco Esteban, the Latin heartthrob. Unfortunately, he is in a bad mood...

SUSAN: **Paco Esteban, los rumores dicen que tienes una nueva amante.**	Paco Esteban, rumor is that you have a new lover.
PACO ESTEBAN: **¿Qué carajos te importa?**	Why the fuck do you care?
SUSAN: **Entonces, ¿no es verdad?** (confused)	Then, it's not true?
PACO ESTEBAN: **Joder, que no es problema tuyo ni de la madre de nadie.**	Damn it, it isn't any of your business, or anybody's mother's.
SUSAN: **Pero, Paco Esteban, no es para tanto.**	But, Paco Esteban, it's not a big deal.
PACO ESTEBAN: **¿De verdad; no me jodas?** (with a sarcastic tone) **Estoy harto de que me hagan la misma puñetera pregunta.**	Really, you don't fucking say? I'm tired of being asked the same fucking question.
SUSAN: **Vaya, disculpa, mejor cambiamos el tema.**	Well sorry, let's change the subject.
PACO ESTEBAN: **Excelente idea.**	Excellent idea.

SUSAN:	¿Quieres enviarles un mensaje a tus fans?	Do you want to send a message to your fans?
PACO ESTEBAN:	Sí, que los amo, aunque sean unos gilipollas. ¡Chao!	Yes, that I love them, even though they're all dumb asses. Ciao!
SUSAN:	Eres un mal hablado.	You're a potty mouth.

Word Bytes

¿De verdad; no me jodas?	Really, you don't fucking say?
puñetero♂/puñetera♀	*Use this adjective the same way as fucking. It has no literal translation.*
¿Qué carajos te importa?	Why the fuck do you care?
Eres un mal hablado♂/ una mal hablada♀.	You're a potty mouth.

Use It or Lose It!

Susan's interview was censored by Unimundo. Exchange the *bips* with Paco Esteban's curses.

SUSAN:	Paco Esteban, los rumores dicen que tienes una nueva amante.
PACO ESTEBAN:	¿Qué -bip- te importa?
SUSAN:	Entonces, ¿no es verdad?
PACO ESTEBAN:	-Bip-, que no es problema tuyo ni de la madre de nadie.
SUSAN:	Pero, Paco Esteban, no es para tanto.
PACO ESTEBAN:	-Bip- Estoy harto de que me hagan la misma –bip- pregunta.
SUSAN:	Vaya, disculpa, mejor cambiamos el tema.
PACO ESTEBAN:	Excelente idea.
SUSAN:	¿Quieres enviarles un mensaje a tus fans?
PACO ESTEBAN:	Sí, que los amo, aunque sean unos –bip-. ¡Chao!

carajos, joder, ¿De verdad; no me jodas?, puñetera, gilipollas

Use It or Lose It!

Think of this as the R-rated version of the Sunday crossword puzzle.

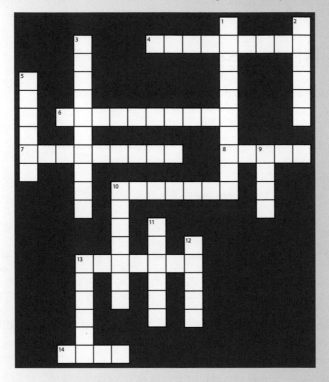

Across

4 say this instead of *jodienda*
6 potty mouth ♂
7 offspring of a bad woman
8 you can drink it or marry in it
10 *Me importa tres* ____
13 butt hair
14 *Me* _____ *en tu madre.*

Down

1 a Spanish dick
2 cheese, milk and meat or a sorry boyfriend
3 cleaner substitution for *cojones*
5 Mexican version of *maldito*
9 female genital organ
10 soccer has one, a *cabrón* has two
11 another way to say shit
12 a sexually explicit verb
13 a vulgar act, solo

Across: 4. chavienda; 6. mal hablado; 7. hijoeputa; 8. leche; 10. carajos; 13. pendejo; 14. cago
Down: 1. gilipollas; 2. cabrón; 3. pantalones; 5. pinche; 9. coño; 10. cojones; 11. mierda; 12. joder; 13. puñeta

You're not gonna find the typical terms in this dictionary, but you will find all of the cool terms, slanguage and swear words used in this book, and then some. Other things you should note:

- Who says a dictionary has gotta be A to Z? This one is Z to A!
- Don't know if a noun is feminine or masculine? If it says el it's masculine, la and it's feminine. There are a few exceptions. Don't worry; we'll let you know!
- Look for ♂/♀ to figure out how to gender-bend adjectives.

zit   el grano 79, el barrito (slang) 119

zipper   la tiendita (slang) 71, la jaula (open fly) 71

your   tu 29, 31, 33, 34, 35, 40, 44, 45, 47, 48, 49, 50, 51, 63, 66, 74, 77, 78, 82, 98, 110, 116, 117, 118, 121, 122

you   tú (informal) 26, 34, 42, 47, 51, usted (formal) 26

yeah right   si claro 60

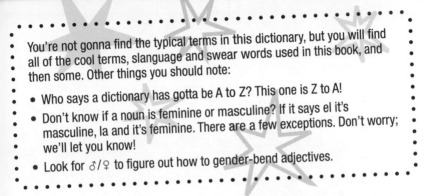

wrinkle   la arruga 77, 78

wireless   inalámbrico ♂/inalámbrica ♀ 59, 66, 88

wine   el vino 76, 87

window   la ventana 75

wife   la mujer (old-fashioned) 25

why   por qué 41, 42, 52, 71, 93, 106, 119

who   quién (as a question or exclamation) 20, 21, 79, 80

whiny	quejón♂/quejona♀ 23
what	que (relative pronoun) 21, 27, 33, 34, 35, 43, 44, 49, 52, 55, 56, 57, 60, 63, 66, 69, 74, 83, 85, 88, 93, 96, 97, 98, 101, 108, 110, 119, 120, 121, qué (as a question or exclamation) 7, 8, 9, 11, 12, 20, 21, 22, 23, 30, 31, 32, 34, 35, 36, 37, 41, 42, 47, 52, 53, 63, 69, 71, 72, 73, 74, 75, 76, 82, 88, 89, 92, 93, 98, 103, 106, 108, 113, 116, 117, 118, 119, 120, 121
website	el sitio web 47, 48, 53, la página web 48, la web 55, el lugar web 48, el website 48
web	la red 49
weather	el tiempo 92
water	el agua♀ 45, 81, 82
watch	el reloj 65, 70
want, to	querer 34
wallet	cartera (in Puerto Rico, a purse) 98

vomit, to	vomitar 79
volume	el volumen 65, 108
voicemail	el buzón de voz 60, 66
view	la vista 88

videogame console	la consola de juegos 61

videogame	el videojuego 61, 88, 89
video player	el reproductor de vídeo 60, 61
video	el vídeo, el video 51, 56, 57, 60, 61, 62, 63, 65, 67, 88, 89
versatile	versátil 31
vajayjey (vagina)	la arepa 38, la tota 38, la concha (slang) 38
vacation	la vacación 102

U

use, to	usar 51, 81, 88
upload, to	cargar 56, 57, subir 49
undress, to	desnudarse 39
undershirt	la camisilla 69, 70
underpants	el calzoncillo 70
un-cool	porquería (garbage) 11, 49, 56, 57, 63, 66, 71, 106, 110, menudo♂/menuda♀ (literally, doesn't measure up) 10, 11, charro♂/charra♀ (lame) 11, la charrería (thing) 11

twice   dos veces 112

TV   la televisión 76

tuxedo   el traje 69, 70, 72

T-shirt   la camiseta 12, 13, 70, 72, 115

true   verdadero ♂/verdadera ♀ 21, 63, 75, 105, 110

transvestite   el/la travesti 27, la draga (drag queen) 27, 28, 31

tourist   el/la turista 91

tongue   la lengua 53

top   el tope (as in the top of a mountain) 76

tomorrow   la mañana 35, 111

toe   el dedo 49

tit   la teta 💣※ 38

tie   la corbata (accessory) 70, 72

ticket   la taquilla (movie) 107

thunder, to   tronar 92

threesome   el trío 44

thanks   gracias 12, 13, 52, 88, 93

text, to   enviar un mensaje de texto 60

testicles   las bolas (balls) 38, las pelotas 💣※ 38

terror   el terror 106

tell, to   decir 116

tacky   charro ♂/charra ♀ 11, de mal gusto 74, 75, 76, cursi (in a romantic sense) 41, 42, 43, 44

table   la mesa 75, 76

sync, to   sincronizar 66

sweetie   chulo ♂/chula ♀ (it also means pimp) 7, 9, 13, 19

suspense   el suspenso 106

surf (the net), to   navegar 49

sure	seguro ♂/segura ♀ 20, 34, 35, 49, 88, 98, 104
sunglasses	las gafas de sol 72
suck, to	mamar 39
stretch, to	estirar 77
stress	el estrés 77, 78
story	el cuento 20
store	la tienda 102, 103
STD	las enfermedades transmitidas sexualmente (ETS) 79
spinster	el aguacatón ♂/la aguacatona ♀ (literally, avocado) 15, el jamón ♂/la jamona ♀ (literally, ham) 15, 16, 23

speaker	bocinas 61, 67
spasm, to have a (neck)	tener un mono trepado 77, 78
Spanish	el español 28, 53, 64, 65, 101, 104
song	la canción 65, 66
son of a bitch	hijo de puta ♂/hija de puta ♀ 💣* 114, 116, 119, 120, hijoeputa (the typical pronounciation) 💣*💣* 119, 122

sofa	el sofá 75, 76
soda	la soda 94, 106, 107
sock	la media 69, 70
soccer	el fútbol 95, 96, 119
soap opera	la telenovela 33, 112, la novela (abbreviation) 108
snob	el niño/la niña bien 16, el/la comemierda 💣* 115, 119

smog	el esmog 82
sleep together, to	acostarse 39
skirt	la falda 29, 70, 71, 73
skinny, to be	estar flaco ♂/flaca ♀ 93
skinny	flaco ♂/flaca ♀ 93
skin	los cueros (literally, leather) 71, 73
sister	la hermana 24, 29, 74, 81, 85, 86, 104
sincerely	sinceramente 19
sick, to be	estar enfermo 79, 80
shut up, to	callarse 106
shop, to	ir de compras 101
shoe repair store	la zapatería 103

shoe	el zapato 70, 71, 72, 73
shit, to	cagarse 💣※ 79, 80, 113, 116, 117, 118, 119, 122
shit	la mierda 💣※💣※ 66, 79, 80, 81, 82, 106, 107, 113, 114, 115, 119, 120, 122

shirt	la camisa 69, 70, 71, 72
share, to	compartir 56, 57
sexy	sexy 52, 53, 55, 71, 102
sex	el sexo 39, 40
serenade	la serenata 41
send, to	enviar 47, 48, 49, 50, 64, 66, 121
see, to	ver 10, 35, 36, 37, 51, 52, 53, 69, 77, 104
search, to	buscar 50, 53, 54, 56, 63, 78
sea	el mar 88
screwed, to be	estar jodido 💣※💣※ 82, 119
scared	asustado ♂/asustada ♀ 19
sale	la rebaja 101, la venta 101, el especial 101
sad	triste 106

rum	el ron 94
rub, to	sobar 39
room	la habitación 74, 75, 88, 89, el cuarto 75
romance	el romance 106
rocker	el rockero ♂/ la rockera ♀ 23

rock (music)	el rock 95, 104, 105
rip off, to	timar 101
right now	ahora mismo 47, 101
ridiculous	ridículo ♂/ridícula ♀ 23, 71, 73
rich, to be	ser rico (official) 99, 100, estar forra'o de dinero (to be covered in money) 99, 100, tener la billetera gorda (to have a fat wallet) 99

reuse, to	volver a usar 81
relaxed	tranquilo ♂/tranquila ♀ 37
relax, to	relajarse 77, 78
reggaeton	el reguetón (a Caribbean type of hip-hop) 95, 96, 104, 105
recycle, to	reciclar 81
receive, to	recibir 31, 40, 64
ready	listo ♂/lista ♀ (listo also means clever, ingenious) 34, 35, 37, 104,
rain, to	llover 92

question	la pregunta 88, 120, 121

purse	el bolso 89, la cartera 98
program	el programa 49, 64, 108
profile	el perfil 47, 53, 54, 59
privacy	la privacidad 53, 54
printer	la impresora 61, 62

print, to	imprimir 48, 49
pride	el orgullo 31, 32, 33
preppy	blanquito ♂/blanquita ♀ (literally, whitey; it can be a noun) 15
popcorn	las palomitas de maíz 106, 107
poor	pobre 99
pool	la piscina 84, 88, 89
play (theater)	la obra de teatro 110
plantain	el plátano 94
pinch, to	pellizcar 45
pimp	el chulo/la chula 9
pill	el anticonceptivo (birth control) 79, 80
pick-up line	el piropo 36, 37
pick up, to (something)	recoger 34, 119
pharmacy	la farmacia 102
peso (currency)	el peso mexicano 97; el peso cubano 97, el peso convertible 97, el CUC (Cuba) 97; el peso colombiano 97, el billete (slang) (Colombia) 97; el peso chileno 97, el billullo (slang) (Chile) 97; el peso argentino 97, los mangos (slang) (Argentina) 97
personality	la personalidad 16, 17
people	la gente 85
penis	el pajarito (literally, birdie) 38
pay, to	pagar 97

password	el contraseña 47, 48, 49, 50
party	la fiesta 12, 13, 16, 17, 72

partner (friend)	el socio/la socia 15, el/la asere (Cuba) (literally partner or associate) 15, el/la pana (Puerto Rico) 15

panty	la braga 69, 70, 102

pants	los pantalones 68, 70, 71, 72, 117, 118, 122
painting	el cuadro (art on display) 74, 75, 76, 102

outfit	el atuendo 69, 70, 72
ouch	auch 116
online	en línea 47, 48, 49, 58

OMG	¡Dios mío! 20
old-fashioned	tradicional 23
old	viejo ♂/vieja ♀ 24, 25, 26
offer	la oferta 101
offended	ofendido ♂/ofendida ♀ 9
OK	vale 34, 35, 36, 51, 104, 113

nudist	el/la nudista 86
no big deal	no es para tanto 120, 121
nipples	las tetillas 38
nice	majo ♂/maja ♀ (Spain) 17
nervous	nervioso ♂/nerviosa ♀ 37
nerd	el nerdo/la nerda 50, 59, 66, 118
neighbor	el vecino/la vecina 20, 22
necklace	el collar 70
neck	el cuello 78

music	la música 16, 17, 49, 60, 61, 65, 67, 95, 103, 104
museum	el museo 85, 86
muscle	el músculo 77
much	mucho ♂/mucha ♀ 16, 17, 82, 88, 89

MP3 player   el toca mp3 61

movie   la película 12, 13, 33, 65, 86, 106, 107

mouth   la boca 78

mouse   el ratón (animal and technological) 60, 61, 62, 66

motherfucker   cabrón ♂/cabrona ♀ 💣✳ 9, 10, 13, 14, 52, 53, 66, 71, 92, 96, 113, 114, 115, 116, 119, 120, 122

money   el dinero (official) 97, la lana (Mexico) 97, la plata (Latin America) 97, los chavos (Caribbean) 97, 98, los cocos (literally coconuts, used ironically) 97, el menudo (coins, slang) 97

mom   la mamá 23

mirror   el espejo 71, 73, 74, 75

microwave   el microondas 67

mess   el reguero 119

melons   los melones (breasts, fruit) 38, las tetas (breasts) 💣✳ 38

me   mí 31, 33, 81

masturbate, to   tocarse (touch oneself) 39, hacerse una paja 💣✳ 39, hacerse una manuela 💣✳ (slang) 39

martial arts   las artes marciales 106

marry, to   casarse 117, 118

many	muchos ♂/muchas ♀ 88, 89
make love, to	hacer el amor (literal translation) 39, hacerlo (slang) 💣✳ 39, 40, 44, 45
make it, to (reach a goal)	lograrlo 60

luggage	valija (South America) 89, 90; petaca (Mexico; be careful, *petacas* also means butt cheeks) 89, 90, 91; el equipaje 89, 90, la maleta (Spain, South America, Puerto Rico, Dominican Republic, Cuba) 89, 90, 91
luck	la suerte 19, 44, 45, 103, 119
lover	el/la amante 42, 44, 45, 46, 120, 121
love, to	amar 41, 42, 43, 121

love	el amor 19, 20, 39, 41, 42, 45, 47, 50, 77, 78

loudspeaker	el altavoz 64, 66
log out, to	cerrar la sesión 49, 54
listen, to	oír 34, 88

liquor	el licor 16, 17

link	el enlace 47, 48, 48, 50, 51
lingerie	la ropa íntima 103

life	la vida 19, 20
lie	la mentira 20
less	menos 52

lesbian	la lesbiana (official) 27, 32, la cachapera 27, 29, la buchs (Puerto Rico) 27, la tortillera (Ecuador) 💣☀ 27, 28, 30

lazy	holgazán ♂/holgazana ♀ 111, 112, vago ♂/vaga ♀ 111
lay down, to	acostarse 39
ladies' night	la noche de damas 95

kitchen	la cocina 74, 75, 76
kiss, to	besarse 39, besuquearse (kiss all over) 39, 40, grajearse (French kiss) 39
kiss	el beso 19, 52, 53

kid	el pibe (slang) 24, el chamo/la chama (Venezuela) 14, 17, el chaval/la chavala (Spain) 24, el carajillo/la carajilla (Venezuela) 24, 25, el chamaco/la chamaca (Puerto Rico) 24, el chavo (Mexico) 24, 25, el mocoso/la mocosa ♀ (literally, full of snot) (Argentina) 24

keyboard	el teclado 60, 61, 64, 66

keep cool, to (stay calm)	mantener la calma 9, 12

jungle	la selva 85, 86
juice	el jugo 88, 89, 94
jewelry shop	la joyería 102, 103
jerk	desgraciado ♂/desgraciada ♀ 42, 43
jeans	los jeans (South America) 70, 71, 73, los mahones (the Caribbean) 70, 72, los vaqueros (Spain) (jeans) 13, 70, 71, 72

issue   el problema 120, 121

iPod®   la iPod® 62, 66, 67, el toca mp3 61

invite, to   invitar 35, 36, 44, 96, 104

invitation   la invitación 12, 13

internet surfer   el/la internauta 49, 50

internet   el/la Internet (this term is bisexual) 48, 49, 63, 88, 89

indifferent   indiferente 37

inconvenient   inconveniente 60

in, to be   estar pega'ó♂/peg'á♀ 96

ignore, to   ignorar 66

I   yo 23, 31, 36, 42, 47, 93, 98, 104

husband   el marido 25, 42

hurt, to   hacer daño 83

hurt   doler 36, 79

hungry, to be   estar muriéndose del hambre (literally, to be dying of hunger) 93

how   cómo (as a question or exclamation) 20, 29, 30, 34, 50, 52, 56, 57, 92, 115

hottie   alguien que está bien bueno (literally, someone who is very good) 36, 37, el papi/la mami (literally, daddy/mommy) 14, 17

hotel   el hotel 85, 86, 88, 89

hot   caliente (note that sometimes *calor* is used when in English hot would be used, for example: it's hot translates to *hace calor*) 81

horror   el horror 106

horrible   espantoso 71, 73

horoscope   el horóscopo 44

home   el hogar 76, la casa (house) 12, 13, 74, 75, 87, 90, inicio (techno lingo) 53, 54

hit   un éxito (as in movie blockbuster) 106

high heel (shoe)   el tacón 70, 72

hello   hola 10, 34, 36, 47, 50, 55, 63, 74, 89

heat   el calor 82, 92

heart   el corazón 19, 20, 41

hear, to   escuchar 21, 63, 66, 104

headphones   los audífonos 61, 62, 102

head   la cabeza (official) 77, 78, 79, 102

have, to   tener 35, 39, 45, 56, 57, 66, 71, 73, 76, 77, 79, 80, 82, 88, 89, 93, 96, 98, 99, 100, 116, 120, 121

hate, to   odiar 41, 42, 43, 52, 66, 79, 81, 85

hardware store   la ferretería 102

happen, to   pasar 21, 22

hangover   la resaca 79, 80

handsome   guapo ♂/guapa ♀ 35, 36, 69

hand luggage   el equipaje de mano 89

hand   la mano 39, 89, 100, 102

guy   el chico (official) 17, 55, 67, 104, el tipo (slang) 14, 20, 26, el chamo (Venezuela) 14, 17, el tío (Spain) 14, 17, 23, 88, 92

guest   el/la huésped 88, 89

greeting   el saludo 9, 36, 54, 62, 90, 105, 112

green, to be   ser verde 81, 83

great   fantástico 68, 110

grandpa   el abuelo 23, abuelito 25

grandma   la abuela 23, 98, abuelita 12, 16, 17, 25

gothic   gótico ♂/gótica ♀ 23

gossip (person)   el chismoso/la chismosa 20

gossip   el chisme 20, 21, 22, el bochinche 20, 22

gorgeous	precioso ♂/preciosa ♀ 36
goody two-shoes	el niño/la niña bien 16
go out, to	salir 29, 34, 35, 36, 44, 64, 69, 77
go on a cruise, to	ir de crucero 84, 86
glasses	las gafas 72, los espejuelos (eyeglasses) 23, las gafas de sol (sunglasses) 72
give, to	dar 31, 32, 77, 78, 101, 108
girlfriend	la novia 20
girl	la nena (slang) 20

get out, to	largarse 41
genre	el género 104
gay	el/la gay 27, el maricón/la maricona (feminine form, though, isn't common, *marimacha* is preferred) 27, 28, el farifo/la farifa (feminine form, though, isn't common) (Puerto Rico) 27, el pato/la pata (literally, duck; Venezuela, Puerto Rico, Nicaragua) 27, 30, el muxe (Mexico) ●❈ 28

garbage	la basura 108
game	el juego 61, 65, 95
gal	la chica (official) 17, 67, 68, 95, la tipa (slang, a bit vulgar) 14, la chama (Venezuela) 14, la tía (Spain) 14, 17

F

funny	cómico ♂/cómica ♀ 107, comiquísimo ♂/ comiquísima ♀ (super funny) 106
full, to be	tener tremenda hartera (to be really fed up) 93, estar harto (to be fed up, too full) 120, 121
fuck, to	joder 92, 113, 114, 119, 120, 121, 122, follar (Spain) 39, 43, coger (to grab or to take—with sexual implications, in some Spanish-speaking countries) 39, echar un polvo (to ejaculate) ●❈●❈ 39

fruit	la fruta 94
friends with benefits	amigos con beneficios 42, 43
friend	el amigo/la amiga (look under partner for more) 12, 13, 31, 33, 36, 42, 43, 45, 53, 54, 86

fridge	el refrigerador 76
fondler	el manisuelto/la manisuelta (can also mean that he/she likes to hit) 35, 37
free	gratis 88, 89, 95, 115
forgetful	algarete 23
foot	el pie 83
flu	el catarrón 79, 80
fitting room	el probador 70
finish, to	acabar (sexual implications, in some Spanish-speaking countries) 39
finger	el dedo 49
fine	bueno ♂/buena ♀ 36, 37
fed up, to be	estar harto 120, 121
fart, to	tirarse un pedo 80
fan	el abanico 100, 102
family	la familia 12, 13, 16, 17, 23, 74, 84, 86, 87

false	falso ♂/falsa ♀ 21, 63, 75, 105, 110
face	la cara 35, 79

eyeglasses	los espejuelos (Caribbean) 23
eye	el ojo 78
exercise	el ejercicio 78
excellent	excelente 110, 120, 121
euro (currency)	el euro 97, 100, las pesetas (out-of-circulation currency, used as slang) 97, el duro (slang) (Spain) 97
environment	el ambiente 81, 82, 83
entrance	la entrada 95
enjoy, to	disfrutar 44, 45, 88
enjoy your meal	buen provecho 93
English	el inglés (language) 58
enable, to	abilitar 49
e-mail	el correo electrónico 47, 48, 49, 50, 59, 60, 66, 120
elegant	elegante 71
electronic (music)	el tecno 95
eat, to	repetir (to have seconds) 93
earring	el arete (hoop) 102

DVD player	el reproductor de DVD 60, 61

dumbass	el bobo-tonto/la boba-tonta (less offensive) 15, 17, el pendejo/la pendeja 💣❋💣❋ 113, 114, 115, 116, 119, 122, el mamao/la mamona 💣❋ 115, 116, el/la gilipollas (Spain) 💣❋ 15, 19, 115, 119, 121, 122

dudette	la tipa 14, la chama (Venezuela) 14, la tía (Spain) 14, 17

dude	el tipo 14, 26, el chamo (Venezuela) 14, 17, el tío (Spain) 14, 17, 88, 92

drunk	el borrachón/la borrachona 15, 16, 17
drop a call, to	cortarse 63, 66

drooler	el baboso/la babosa 42
drink	el trago (alchohol) 36, 86, 95, 96
dressing room	el probador 71
dress	el vestido 70, 71, 72, 73, 102
drama	el drama 106
download, to	descargar 49
dollar	el dólar americano (used as currency in Puerto Rico, Panama, Ecuador, Costa Rica) 97, los pesos (slang) (Puerto Rico) 97, el billuzo (slang) (Ecuador) 97
do, to	hacer 31, 32, 34, 35, 37, 39, 40, 44, 45, 77, 78, 82, 98
do it, to	hacerlo (a synonym for sex) 💣❋ 39, 40, 44, 45
disgusting	fo 79, 80, 81, 93, qué asco 93, guácatela (phrases to express disgust) 93
digital camera	la cámara digital 60, 61

diarrhea, to have	estar de carreritas (slang) 79
delicious	delicioso ♂/deliciosa ♀ 93

delete, to	borrar 48
dear	querido ♂/querida ♀ 9, 19, 20, 26, 32, 37, 41, 54, 62, 90, 96, 105, 112, 115
day	el día 92, 108
date	la cita 34, 36, 37, 45, 47, 55
darling	cariño ♂/♀ 19, 20
dance, to	bailar 96, 104, perrear (if it's *reguetón* we're talking about) 96
dance	el baile 16, 17
damn, to	maldecir 115, 119
damn	maldito ♂/maldita ♀ 63, 85, pinche (Mexico) 88, 115, 119, 122, maldición (single curse word) 💣✳ 66, 115, carajo (single curse word) 💣✳💣✳ 116, 117
dad	el papá 23

cunt	el coño (mainly used as a single word curse) 💣✳ 63, 82, 88, 113, 115, 116, 117, 119, 122
crotch	el paquete (literally, package) 38

critic	el crítico/la crítica 107
crazy	loco ♂/loca ♀ 31, 32, 77, 78, 106, 107
crappy	porquería 11, 49, 56, 57, 63, 71, 106, 110
crack	la alcancía 68, 73, la raja (butt crack) 71
cover	el tape 31, 33
cousin	el primo/la prima 23
couple	los novios 42, 43
corner	la esquina 12, 13
cool (exclamation or state of being)	cool 9, 10, 12, 23, 53, 89, 104, 106, chévere 7, 8, 9, 10, 13, espectacular 7, 13, 71, 72, tremendo ♂/tremenda ♀ 7, 8, 10, 36, 79, 80, 93, impresionante 8, 10, estupendo 8, chulin 8, 9, chulo ♂/chula ♀ 7, 8, 9, 10, demasiado (literally, too much) 8, 9, 35, 81, 110, guay (Spain) 8, 10, 12, 13, 17, 47, 88, 89, brutal (Puerto Rico) 8, 12, 13, 56, 57, 69, 85, 104, bacán (Peru) 8, padre (literally, father) (Mexico) 8, 10, chimba (Honduras) 8, bacano ♂/bacana ♀ (Colombia) 8, 10, legal (Argentina) 8
contact	nombre 64
connected (online)	conectado ♂/conectada ♀ 47, 48, 67
condom	el condón 79

concubine	el marinovio/la marinovia 42, 43
concert	el concierto 104, 110, 119
computer	el computador (South America) 61, el ordenador (Spain) 61, 62, la computadora (the Caribbean) 59, 60, 61, 62, 66, 67, la computadora portátil (laptop) 61

commercial ballad	la balada-pop 105
comic strip	las tirillas cómicas 111, 112
comfortable	cómodo♂/cómoda♀ 74, 77, 78
comedy	la comedia 106
come, to	venirse (with or without sexual implications) 39
color	el color 44, 45
colon (currency)	el colon 97, las lucas (slang) (El Salvador) 97, el colón costarricense 97, las cañas (slang) (Costa Rica) 97
cold	frío♂/fría♀ 7, 92
coffee	el café 82

cock	la verga ◆✳◆✳ 38, el pajarito (funny way of saying it) 38, el bicho (Puerto Rico) ◆✳◆✳ 38
coat	el abrigo 70
clothing	la ropa 81, 103, 119
closet	el clóset 29, 30
close, to	cerrar 49, 53, 54
clock	el reloj 65, 70
click, to	hacer click 48

check, to	chequear 47, 48
chat, to	chatear 47, 48, 51, 52, 53
change, to	cambiar 63, 71, 10, 121
chandelier	el candelabro 75
chair	la silla 75
center	el centro 85, 88, 89
cell phone	el teléfono celular 61, 66, el móvil 51, 60, 61, 62, 63, 64, 66, 67, 88, 89

carpool	el aventón 82
care, to	importar 101, 104, 117, 118, 120, 121, 122
car	el carro 11, 22, 83
candle	la vela 75
cancel, to	cancelar 49
camping, to go	acampar 72
call, to	llamar 35, 37, 64
call	la llamada 35, 64, 66

buy, to	comprar 49, 101, 102
button	el botón 49
butt cheek	la nalga 38, 71, 73
butt	el culo 38, 44, 45, 96

but	pero 10, 44, 45, 49, 51, 60, 68, 69, 84, 98, 104, 107, 120, 121
busy	ocupado ♂/ocupada ♀ 35
business	el negocio 88, 89
buns	las nalgas (butt cheeks) 38, 71, 73
brother	el hermano 20, 23, 24
broke, to be	estar en la prángana (slang) 98, 99, 100, estar pela'o (literally, to be peeled) 98, 99, 100, no tener ni un centavo (to have not even a cent) 98, 99, 100
breast	la teta (slang) 💣💧 38
bra	el sostén 69, 70
boyfriend	el novio 42, 85, 86
bottom	abajo (of something) 31, el fondillo (meaning ass) 38
boring	aburrido ♂/aburrida ♀ 110
boot	la bota 70
bookworm	el/la comelibros 111, 112
bookstore	la librería 102, 103
bookshelf	el librero 75
boliviano (currency)	el boliviano 97, el peso (slang) (Bolivia) 97
body	el cuerpo 68
Blu-ray player	el reproductor de Blu-ray 61

blouse	la blusa 68, 70, 71, 72
bloggers	los blogueros 55
blind date	la cita a ciegas 55
bitch	la puta 113, 114, 115, 116, 119, 120, el puto (male version) 💣💣 115
bisexual	bisexual (official) 27, 30, 32, estereosexual (literally, stereosexual) 27, la/el que pinta y raspa (literally, the one who paints and scrapes) (slang) 💣 27
bike	la bici (abbreviation) 83, 88, 89
best	mejor (adjective) 31, 33, 76, 96, 119, 120, 121, el/la mejor (noun) 23, 55, 56, 104, el más cabrón ♂/ la más cabrona ♀ (noun) 💣 96
belt	la correa 69, 70, el cinturón 70
beer	la cerveza 94, 95

beep	el bip (sound) 63, 121
bedroom	el dormitorio 75
bed	la cama 45, 74, 75, 76
because	porque 52, 119

beautiful	hermoso ♂/hermosa ♀ 71
bear	el oso (animal; also, gay) 31
beach	la playa 12, 13, 17, 74, 85, 86
battery	la batería 60, 66
bathing suite	el bañador 68, 70, 72
bar	la barra 31, 32, 66, 86, 88, 89, 95
band	la banda (as in rock) 95
balls	las bolas 38, las pelotas 💣 (when used as male anatomy) 38
bag	la bolsa (as in paper or plastic) 81, 82, 83, 89, el bolso (purse) 89

bad words	malas palabras 113, 115, 116
bad	malo ♂/mala ♀ 10, 113, 115, 116, fatal (so bad it might kill you) 71, 110
backpacking	ir de mochilero ♂/ mochilera ♀ 85, 86
back	atrás (position) 39, 40, 64, la espalda (body part) 79

A

awesome	tremendo ♂/tremenda ♀ 7, 8, 10, 36, 79, 80, 93
aunt	la tía (formal) 23, la titi (diminutive) 25
atmosphere	el ambiente 95
asshole	el pendejo/la pendeja (literally, a hair in the ass) 💣✱💣✱ 113, 114, 115, 116, 119, 122
ass	el culo 💣✱💣✱ 38, 44, 45, 96
ask, to	preguntar 88, 120, 121
artist	el/la artista 65
art	el arte 102, 103, 106
archaic	arcaico ♂/arcaica ♀ 51

appliance	el enser 74, 76
apartment	el apartamento 20, 74, 75, el piso (Spain) 75
anything	cualquier cosa 12, 13
amenities	las amenidades 88
ambiguous	ambiguo ♂/ambigua ♀ 31, 32
affair	el lío de faldas 29
adventure	la aventura 44, 85
address	la dirección 48, 49, 85
action	la acción 106
achy	achacoso ♂/achacosa ♀ 23
account	la cuenta 47, 48, 50, 53, 54, 56, 59
accessory	el accesorio 70
a lot	mucho ♂/mucha ♀ 16, 17, 45, 52, 53, 82, 88, 89